Women, Work, and Divorce

SUNY Series in the Sociology of Work

Judith R. Blau and *Robert L. Kaufman*, Editors

Women,
Work,
and
Divorce

RICHARD R. PETERSON

State University of New York Press

Published by
State University of New York Press, Albany

For information, address State University of New York
Press, State University Plaza, Albany, N.Y., 12246

Library of Congress Cataloging-in-Publication Data

Peterson, Richard R., 1955–
    Women, work, and divorce.

    (SUNY series in the sociology of work)
    Bibliography: p.
    Includes index.
    1. Divorced women—United States—Economic conditions.
2. Divorced women—Employment—United States. 3. Labor
supply—United States. I. Title. II. Series.
HQ834.P48   1988   306.8'9   88–2133
ISBN 0-88706-858-8
ISBN 0-88706-859-6 (pbk.)

10 9 8 7 6 5 4 3 2 1

Contents

List of Tables

List of Figures

Acknowledgments

Many colleagues and friends have made important contributions to my work on this book.

The editors at SUNY Press did a wonderful job of supporting my work from its initial review to final publication. Judith Blau, a co-editor of this series in the Sociology of Work, was the first to recognize the potential of my dissertation manuscript for publication as a book. She reviewed several drafts of the manuscript and provided valuable suggestions for revisions. She also provided encouragement when problems seemed intractable, and a gentle push when progress was slow. Robert Kaufman, a co-editor of the series, offered useful comments about the statistical analyses and the discussion of labor market segmentation. Several anonymous reviewers pointed out weaknesses in the study and made suggests for improvement. Rosalie Robertson provided encouragement and technical advice.

My colleagues in the Department of Sociology at New York University helped me to develop my ideas and offered moral support along the way. Kathleen Gerson, Barbara Heyns, Robert Jackson, and Beth Stevens provided advice and comments which improved the quality of the manuscript. Thanks to Theresa Schoenacher for her able assistance with the data analyses in Appendix D.

I also owe a large debt to the professors and students at Columbia University who commented on this manuscript while it was in draft as a dissertation: Joseph Altonji, Ellen Auster, Peter M. Blau, Linda Cranor, Eric Hirsch, Yvette Schlussel, Joseph Schwartz, and Viviana Zelizer. The assistance of Carl Pieper in making data available from the Quality of Employment Surveys is also appreciated.

The funds required for computer analyses were provided by Columbia University and New York University.

Finally, I would like to acknowledge the contributions of Rita Duffy. Without her I might never have become interested in the study of gender inequality or of women's work careers. She suffered with me while I was working frantically to complete the manuscript and offered encouragement when I doubted that the work would ever get done. She edited the final manuscript, offering many suggestions to make it more readable. This book is dedicated to her.

CHAPTER 1

Women, Work, and Divorce

1.1 INTRODUCTION

The economic deprivation that women in the United States suffer after divorce is by now well documented. Divorce has become so common, and its economic effects on women are so severe, that it is now considered a major cause of poverty in the United States. Growing numbers of divorced and separated women are unable to earn enough to support themselves and their children. Recent attention has focused on the legal problems encountered by these women, particularly those created by no-fault divorce laws that emphasize the presumption that both men and women ought to be self-supporting after divorce. Research on the economic problems of divorced women in the United States has focused primarily on the "financial catastrophe" in the period immediately following divorce.[1] However, little is known about how women respond to this disaster and how they fare in the long term.

This book finds that over the long run, many divorced women in the United States make at least a partial economic recovery, and it explains the reasons for this recovery. The findings are relevant not only to an understanding of divorce and its consequences, but also to more general issues in the study of changing gender roles, work–family linkages, and the labor market.

High rates of divorce and women's continuing disadvantage in the labor market insure that the economic problems of divorced women will continue to be the subject of policy debates. Although divorce rates have recently leveled off in the United States, they remain high and it is unlikely they will drop significantly.[2] Between 1960 and 1980, the divorce rate increased from 9 per 1,000 married women (age 15 and over) to over 22 per 1,000 married women.[3] Each successive marriage cohort from 1960 to 1973 has experienced higher proportions of marriages eventually ending in divorce than did the previous marriage cohorts.[4] The rising divorce rate, coupled

1

with declining rates of remarriage,[5] has resulted in a sharp rise in the proportion of adult women "currently divorced"—from 2.6% in 1960 to 8.7% in 1985.[6]

Divorced women, like other women, continue to be at a disadvantage in the labor market. The level of occupational segregation by sex, which remained relatively stable before 1970, began a slow decline in the 1970s. In spite of this decline, sex segregation of occupations remains at a high level. About 62% of women would have had to change occupations to eliminate occupational sex segregation in 1981.[7] Furthermore, while the earnings gap between men and women has declined since the early 1970s, a significant gap of about 35% remains.[8] A study of new entrants to the labor force found that women actually fared worse in 1980 than in 1970 when compared to men.[9] With so many women experiencing divorce and facing unfavorable labor market conditions, the economic plight of divorced women continues to be an important issue.

The financial disaster many women experience after divorce suggests that work is becoming increasingly important for married women's economic security. While women in "traditional" marriages rely on their spouses' income, no-fault divorce laws combined with rising divorce rates have substantially increased the risks for women in such marriages.[10] Under no-fault divorce laws, divorced women are now expected to be able to support themselves. This changing expectation regarding divorced women reflects changing expectations regarding women and work. As Lenore Weitzman (1985) has argued, it is unfair for the courts to expect older women who married under the "traditional" rules to be self-supporting. However, the message for younger women is clear. Their economic security over the life cycle depends primarily on their own, not their spouses', earnings. Young women are less able to afford career sacrifices to raise children than were previous generations of women. The cost of these sacrifices for an older cohort of divorced women is clear from the analyses presented in this study.

This study provides a long-term view of how the financial disaster often associated with divorce affects women's work outcomes and economic well-being. The emphasis on long-term versus short-term outcomes represents more than a difference in time perspective, however. Short-term evaluations emphasize the plight of women who have just been divorced, and the role of their spouses and the legal system in creating that plight. To go beyond a description of the immediate problems of divorced women, studies must consider how divorced women respond to the economic deprivation brought about by current legal and economic conditions. While most research has recognized that divorce provides strong economic incentives for women to work, studies have focused almost exclusively on evaluations of the short-term effects of increased work activity. However, the full effects of women's work adjustments after divorce cannot be evaluated until several years later. A long-term evaluation emphasizes the importance of women's work adjustments in response to the economic consequences of divorce.

Research on the economic effects of divorce also provides an opportunity to learn more about how and why family events affect work outcomes. For most people, divorce is a significant, and unexpected, change in the life course affecting both their work and their family situations. Yet women are differentially affected by divorce. A woman's work history and her family history prior to divorce are important determinants of her financial situation after divorce. Women who have continuous work experience and who have few children are likely to be better prepared to support themselves after divorce. Work–family linkages, including the relationship between divorce and work outcomes, should not be considered in isolation, but must be viewed in the context of the life course.

Until recently, the relationships between work and family life were addressed only at the most general level. Rosabeth Kanter argued that this gap in research was due to "the 'myth' of separate worlds," i.e., that the worlds of work and of family are separate from and independent of each other.[11] The myth has since been shattered, as evidenced by the flood of research produced in the last decade on the interrelationships between work and family. This research has been motivated by interest in women's changing roles and in the study of gender inequality, specifically the study of whether and how family responsibilities disadvantage women in the labor market. Nevertheless, many of the connections between work and family remain unexplored.

It is often asserted that women's greater burden of family responsibilities is a major reason for their disadvantaged position in the labor market. While many studies have compared men's and women's labor market outcomes, relatively few have considered variation *among women* in the level of family responsibilities. Those few studies that have considered such variation have generally compared married and never-married women, assuming that the latter lack family responsibilities. These studies find that never-married women fare better than married women, but not nearly as well as men. Divorced women provide an interesting contrast. Their work careers have been affected by family responsibilities during marriage. After divorce, many women continue to have responsibility for caring for children; yet they are also subject to the economic incentives to work experienced by never-married women. Understanding how divorced women cope with these responsibilities and incentives should provide new insight into the relationship between work and family.

This study employs both individualist and structural models to explain the work outcomes of divorced women. The individualist model is based primarily on human capital theory, while the structural model is drawn from a labor market segmentation approach. Although structural models have been applied to the study of various labor market outcomes, they have not yet been extended to the study of the consequences of divorce.

It is generally assumed that the marital status of employees is unrelated to their location in particular labor market segments. However, employers may believe that single women are better employees (i.e., more stable, productive, reliable, etc.) than married women. If so, it may be easier for some single women (e.g., divorced or never married) to obtain jobs in advantaged labor market segments. While the data used here do not measure employer preferences directly, data on labor market segmentation by marital history will be presented. It will be argued that labor market segmentation by marital history is an indirect indicator of an employer preference for single women as employees. Although most prior studies assume that divorce affects work outcomes because of changes in the work behavior of divorced women, this study will also test whether work outcomes of divorced women are affected by their location in particular labor market segments. Finally, while primary attention is focused on how the models perform in accounting for the effects of divorce, the results will also provide a comparative evaluation of the ability of the individualist and the structural approaches to explain labor market outcomes.

This chapter provides an overview of research on the economic consequences of divorce in the context of these broader issues. It reviews research on women's economic well-being after divorce, and considers past research on the relationship between divorce and work outcomes. Finally, it reviews individualist and structural approaches to the study of women's labor market outcomes, and discusses how they will be applied to the study of the effects of divorce.

1.2   THE EFFECT OF DIVORCE ON WOMEN'S ECONOMIC WELL-BEING

Over the past few decades, women have increasingly relied on their own earnings for financial support. Female labor force participation rates have risen steadily, with particularly sharp increases among young women and women who have children, especially among those who have young children.[12] Perhaps more significant than the movement of women into the labor force is the movement of women into some traditionally male occupations. Between 1960 and 1979, the percentage of women workers in certain "male" occupations (e.g., accountant, lawyer, bus driver) rose significantly.[13] Occupational segregation by sex declined in the 1970s and a further modest decline is expected through the 1980s.[14] Changes in women's gender attitudes have accompanied these trends. Women's support for egalitarian gender attitudes increased rapidly in the late 1960s and early 1970s.[15] This trend continued into the 1980s.[16] A national survey showed a sharp decline in the perceived importance of motherhood among American women, relative to the perceived importance of work, between 1970 and 1983.[17]

While women are increasingly relying on their own earnings, it is not reasonable to assume that all married women could be economically self-sufficient in the event of divorce. In spite of their progress, women are not competing equally with men in the labor market. The problems caused by this disparity have been brought into sharp focus by the plight of women divorced in the 1970s and 1980s. Weitzman (1985), in a critical study of the effects of the no-fault divorce law in California, argues that many women fare worse under the new law than under the old fault-based divorce law. The aims of the legal reform, according to Weitzman, were (1) to reduce the antagonistic nature of divorce by eliminating the need for grounds for divorce, (2) to base financial awards on needs and resources rather than on how much blame each party shared for the breakdown of the marriage, and (3) to treat both parties equally, based on gender-neutral rules. Weitzman documents the legal consequences of these changes for women, including fewer alimony awards, a reduction in the amount and duration of alimony awards, and inadequate child support awards.[18] These changes especially hurt mothers of pre-school children, women who had intermittent work patterns during marriage, and older housewives. These women were not prepared to support themselves after divorce, yet judges were interpreting "equal" treatment to mean that both men and women should support themselves after divorce, regardless of their prior work history. Weitzman concludes that the legal presumption of equality did not reflect the constraints faced by divorced women.

Not surprisingly, women suffer a drastic drop in their income and standard of living in the first year after their divorce. This decline is especially severe for women who have children, women who were married to upper middle-class men, and long-married women. Weitzman found that while the average divorced woman experiences a 73% drop in her standard of living, divorced men experience a 42% *increase*.[19] Even after making alimony and child support payments, divorced men have more disposable income after divorce than before divorce. Women of all social classes are likely to experience not only relative deprivation (in comparison to their spouses) but also severe economic hardship after divorce. Weitzman argues that divorce is a major cause of the impoverishment of women and children and that "we may well arrive at a two-tier society with an underclass of women and children."[20]

Other studies, based on national samples, confirm Weitzman's conclusions regarding the short-term economic plight of women after divorce. The income of women is much lower after divorce or separation. It is widely acknowledged that divorce is more common among low-income couples.[21] Yet, even after controlling for their initially low income, divorced women are worse off, on average, than women who remain continuously married.[22] One national study, the Panel Study of Income Dynamics, found that fewer than half of divorced women received alimony or child support payments. Even for those who receive them, these payments provide for less than half the basic needs of the mother and children, on average.[23] Divorced women, especially whose who have children, are more likely to become poor than women who remain married, and are more likely to remain poor over a period of years.[24] Working divorced women often do not earn enough to stay out of poverty.[25] For women who have low potential earning power, public assistance or remarriage may be viable alternatives.[26]

While these findings generally confirm those in Weitzman's study, a closer look at research focusing on longer-term outcomes suggests that some women achieve at least a partial recovery from the financial disaster of divorce. Weitzman argues that other studies "found parallel disparities in the standards of living for former husbands and wives after divorce."[27] However, while the studies she cites confirm that husbands' standard of living increased and wives' decreased after divorce, none of these studies found effects as large as those in Weitzman's study. Hoffman and Holmes (1976) report a 7% decline in the standard of living between 1967 and 1973 for women in the Panel Study of Income Dynamics who divorced between those years.[28] Corcoran (1979b), using the same data set but slightly different methods, reports an 18% decline for women divorced between 1967 and 1974. These studies differ from Weitzman's in at least two critical respects. They are based on a representative national sample, while her sample is drawn solely from California. Secondly, and perhaps more important, the studies include women who have been divorced between one and six or seven years, while Weitzman's data pertain only to the first year after divorce. Weitzman's data are unique in that they document a dramatic drop in women's income in the first year after divorce. Studies such as Corcoran's and Hoffman and Holmes' that consider women who have been divorced for longer periods of time, find a less drastic decline in their standard of living. Apparently, women improve their standard of living after that first post-divorce year.

Nestel et al. (1983) traced changes in the standard of living of women who divorced between 1967 and 1977, using data from the National

Longitudinal Surveys of Mature Women. They found roughly a 40% drop in the standard of living by the first interview (not necessarily the first year) after marital dissolution. However, in later interviews, the standard of living of the average divorced woman increased, reaching about 80% of its previous level (i.e., a 20% decline) in 1976. This pattern indicates that divorced women make adjustments to recover from the initial financial disaster caused by divorce.

Divorced women adjust to the financial disaster primarily by increasing their own earnings.[29] This increase is especially strong for women who were middle class or upper middle class before divorce. Weiss (1984) found that separated and divorced single mothers who were in the top two-thirds of the income distribution before marital disruption were increasingly likely to rely on their own earnings for income in the years after the disruption: by five years after divorce, about 70% of the income of these women was derived from their own earnings, on average. Women in the lower third of the income distribution did not increase their reliance on earnings over time: less than 60% of their income, on average, came from earnings five years after divorce. Women in this lower-income group were heavily dependent on public assistance income in the year after divorce, and did not become less so in subsequent years. Yet, while public assistance provides an alternative for some women, most women adjust to the economic hardship caused by divorce by working more hours and improving their earnings capacity. Lois Shaw concludes that "the employment of the woman herself is the major means of avoiding poverty."[30] To understand the economic consequences of divorce for women, one must learn more about the effects of divorce on women's work outcomes.

1.3 THE EFFECT OF DIVORCE ON WOMEN'S POSITION IN THE LABOR MARKET

The two dominant, and competing, approaches in empirical stratification research are human capital theory and labor market segmentation theory. Human capital theory is concerned with how rewards are determined by productivity differences among workers (i.e., supply characteristics), and assumes that demand for labor is determined in a competitive labor market. Labor market segmentation theory assumes that there are institutional barriers that fragment competition, and is concerned with how rewards are determined by structural features of labor markets (i.e., demand characteristics). Segmentation theorists argue that individual characteristics (e.g., human capital) affect rewards only within the constraints of structural features of the labor market. From a sociological point of view, the distinction between these two theories may be viewed as a distinction between *individualist* and *structural* explanations of labor market phenomena.

The effects of marital status on work outcomes are most often considered in the context of human capital models rather than labor market segmentation models. There may be instances in which the labor market affects marital status (e.g., job pressures lead to divorce), or firms use marital status as a job requirement (e.g, flight attendants were once required to be single). However, it is generally assumed that the demand for female labor is indifferent to marital status. As a result of this assumption, most structural models ignore differentiation among women by marital status.

Individualist Approaches. Prior research on the effects of divorce on work outcomes has been based primarily on an individualist approach: human capital, occupational status attainment, and family role variables are considered to account for differences in labor market outcomes between divorced and married women. The fundamental assumption of the individualist approach is that divorce increases the economic incentives for a woman to work. Divorce increases economic need for women, and is presumed to result in increases in labor supply to compensate for the loss of spouse's income. According to human capital theory, women make trade-offs between household labor and market work. Married women specialize in domestic labor (e.g., child care) at the expense of market labor to maximize household efficiency (see later discussion). Divorced and other single women must emphasize market work over domestic labor because of economic need.

Most research has not directly compared married and divorced women, but rather currently and formerly married women.[31] As a result, many of the findings on the effects of divorce are actually based on the experience of all formerly married women (i.e., separated and widowed, as well as divorced women). This imprecision in the measurement of marital status casts doubt on some of the effects attributed to divorce, as will be described later.

Cross-sectional studies have found that formerly married women are more likely to work than currently married women, and work more hours per year. Because they work more hours, formerly married women have higher annual earnings. However, nearly all studies find that the hourly wages of currently and formerly married women are virtually the same.[32] One exception is a study by Salvo and McNeil (1984), who used a more precise measure of marital status. They report that among white females, women who were ever divorced have higher wages than never-divorced married women, even after controlling for education and work experience variables.

While children reduce the labor supply of currently married women, they have no effect on the labor supply of formerly married women.

However, children have a negative effect on earnings of both currently and formerly married women.[33] Hudis (1976) argues that because of economic need, formerly married women who have children give precedence to work (i.e., by working more hours), but that past family responsibilities limit the ability of both currently and formerly married women to earn higher hourly wages.

Research using longitudinal data has focused on short-term effects and has arrived at similar conclusions. The number of hours worked is substantially higher for divorced women than for women who remain continuously married.[34] Even women who have children work more hours after separation or divorce than they did while married.[35] However, in the short run (1 to 2 years), the average wage of working women is actually *lower* after divorce,[36] because many are recent entrants to the labor market. In summary, women seem to respond to divorce by working more hours, resulting in higher annual earnings. However, there is little evidence that they improve their earning power (i.e., hourly wage) after divorce.

Never-married women provide an interesting comparison group for the study of divorced women, since their work careers, presumably, are least affected by family responsibilities.[37] Treiman and Terrell (1975) argue that married women are less likely to be in the labor force than never-married women, because married women are often geographically more restricted than other women, and they are likely to take time off for child rearing. Hudis (1976) argues that the demands of family and work are often incompatible, and that, for married women, cultural prescriptions favor family roles over work roles. Never-married women without children are not subject to the constraints of spouses' attitudes nor limitations on hours or location of work, and therefore can be expected to have higher earnings than married women who have children.

Of course, as Roos (1985) notes, comparisons of married and never-married women must control for age, since many never-married women are young women who plan to marry and whose labor force behavior may be affected by expectations of marriage. Among older women, never-married women are more likely to work, and have more years of education and higher occupational prestige than ever-married women.[38] Their annual earnings and hourly wages are also higher than those of ever-married women, but not nearly as high as those of men.[39] The latter finding indicates that differences in level of family obligations do not entirely (or even largely) account for the differences between male and female earnings.[40] Never-married women, who generally have few family obligations, do not fare nearly as well as men.

Structural Approaches. Studies of labor market influences, for reasons indicated above, generally do not consider marital status differences among women. Two exceptions are studies by Oppenheimer (1970) and Scharf (1980), who have reviewed historical evidence on differential demand for female labor on the basis of marital status. Negative attitudes toward married women working in the 1930s and 1940s were reflected in discriminatory policies toward married women (for example in the teaching profession) and in legislation proposed in 26 states to place restrictions on, or to forbid, married women from working. (Such legislation passed only in Louisiana, and was later repealed.) During the 1950s, the increasing demand for female labor (clerical work and selected professional and service occupations) began to exceed the supply of preferred young single female workers. As a result, employers were forced to hire more married women. Since then, "there has been a general shift away from hiring policies which discriminate against married or older women."[41] Oppenheimer concludes that differences in demand for married and single women had largely disappeared by 1960.

Subsequent research on this subject has been rare. Two studies of sex differences within firms did consider marital status (single versus married) in their models predicting salary.[42] Neither study found a significant direct effect of marital status, after controlling for education and work experience variables. Halaby (1979) found that returns to schooling were 15% higher for single than for married women, but there were no other significant differences in returns to work experience between married and single women. Talbert and Bose (1977) and Bridges and Berk (1974) found that married women earn *more* than single women. The failure of these studies to find an advantage for single women could be due to a failure to adequately control for age (since single workers tend to be younger, and young workers earn less than older workers). In addition, some organizations may prefer married women while others prefer single women, as Siebert and Sloane (1981) found in their study of five British firms. These findings, combined with the historical evidence, suggest that firms' preferences do not account for earnings differences among women on the basis of marital status.

Summary. Theoretical and analytic shortcomings of current research on the effects of divorce on women's work outcomes leave several major issues unresolved. The measures of marital status often group together women who would be expected to have widely different experiences. For example, the economic effects of widowhood might be quite different from those of divorce,[43] yet many studies consider these two groups together as "formerly married." An equally important problem is that the often-used comparison group of "currently married" women includes women who have been divorced or widowed and who have remarried. Such women may differ from other married women in important respects.[44] The importance of this distinction is highlighted by the fact that the one cross-sectional study that found a positive effect of divorce on earnings compared *ever-divorced* women to married *never-divorced* women.[45] Because of these measurement problems, the failure of most previous studies to find differences between currently and formerly married women does not directly address the question of whether divorced women fare better than married women in the labor market.

While cross-sectional and longitudinal studies find that divorced women increase their labor supply, they fail to consider that work adjustments made by divorced women may show an effect on earnings only after a sufficiently long period of time. Most longitudinal research on the effects of divorce has been limited to a relatively short-term evaluation of those effects. One would expect that working women who have been divorced for a long time are more economically secure than recently divorced women.

Attempts to account for earnings differences by marital status among women have generally focused on individualist explanations. No study, however, has tested a well-developed human capital model, i.e., one which includes measures of education, work experience, and tenure at current job. And, although sociologists[46] and some economists[47] have argued that the human capital model needs to be extended to include consideration of family labor supply issues, no study has included family role variables, such as amount of earnings of other workers in the household, gender attitudes, or number of children.

Furthermore, structural approaches have been largely ignored as an explanatory model for marital status differences. The few studies which have been done suggest that demand for female labor no longer differs by marital status. In the literature on wage differences between men and women, however, there is ample discussion of demand factors. Employers view women as "secondary" workers since women's primary role is perceived to be in the family, as wife and mother. While human capital theorists have argued that women specialize in and emphasize their family roles at the expense of their work roles, the "demand"-side researchers argue that this specialization largely reflects employers' expectations of women workers. Because employers give women only secondary jobs, women have placed more emphasis on family roles. Coser and Rokoff (1974) speculate that employers may distinguish between married women (who have family responsibilities) and childless never-married women (who do not). It is also interesting to speculate whether employers differentiate between married women and those who have left marriages (leaving the role of wife, but not necessarily the "mother" role). Of course, as Coser and Rokoff note, employers may expect that unmarried women will eventually marry; hence, employers may view all women as secondary or potentially secondary workers, subject to the constraints of a present or anticipated primary role in the family. Nevertheless, the hypothesized indifference of employers to marital history should be tested, not merely assumed.

1.4   MODELS OF WOMEN'S LABOR MARKET OUTCOMES: INDIVIDUALIST APPROACHES

The research reviewed in the previous section pertains specifically to the relationship between marital status and work. This study attempts to fill a significant gap in that research by considering the long-run effects of divorce on work outcomes, using individualist and structural models. This section and the next review the theoretical underpinnings of these two approaches and their application to the study of women's labor market outcomes. This in-depth review will provide the basis for selecting the explanatory variables to be included in the models developed in later chapters.

There are two related theories that have been used to estimate how and to what extent individual characteristics account for variation in work outcomes: status attainment theory and human capital theory. Status attainment theory, developed primarily by sociologists, attempts to predict occupational status from a worker's education and family background characteristics.[48] Human capital theory, developed primarily by economists, is concerned with predicting wage rates from measures of a worker's productivity, or his/her human capital.[49] While there are differences in emphasis between the two theories, they share some common assumptions: (1) a worker's position in the labor market can be evaluated along a single dimension (i.e., wages, a proxy for productivity, in human capital theory; occupational status in status attainment theory); (2) there is a single labor market within which workers compete for available jobs; (3) within this labor market there is perfect competition, perfect availability of information and perfect opportunity for mobility; (4) workers are rewarded (in terms of wages or occupational status) according to how much human capital they have. When the market is in equilibrium, workers receive rewards exactly equal to their contribution to the firm.[50]

It is interesting to note that while individualist approaches claim to provide comprehensive explanations of gender inequality, they make no such claims for racial inequality. Although it is sometimes argued that blacks have less human capital (education, work experience, or occupational training) than whites, there is no human capital theory of racial inequality. It is generally considered unacceptable to argue that blacks are less productive or reliable than whites, that blacks don't have the ability to perform in certain jobs, or that blacks are less committed to work. It is also unacceptable to argue that blacks work in racially segregated occupations because they choose to do so; nor is it argued that racial inequality can be justified because blacks are socialized differently than whites. Yet each of those arguments has been advanced and developed to justify gender inequality. Theories of racial inequality focus almost exclusively on structural sources of discrimination rather than racial differences in human capital, yet gender inequality is often explained by human capital theories as well as by structural theories. Essentialist arguments concerning gender differences are seriously considered while essentialist arguments concerning racial differences are not. And, with a few exceptions, human capital theory is the only approach used to account for marital history differences among women. Because human capital arguments continue to be important in the theoretical debate about gender inequality, this book will consider such explanations for marital history differences among women. However, to correct for the theoretical imbalance in the discussion of these differences, a structural approach is also developed.

Status Attainment Theory. Most researchers have found that the process of status attainment is essentially similar for men and women.[51] Among married workers in the experienced civilian labor force, women "enjoy more socioeconomic opportunity than do men" insofar as they are (slightly) less influenced by their family background and have (slightly) higher mean education and mean occupational status than men.[52] But the conclusion that the attainment processes for men and women are similar is suspect for several reasons. First, this finding does not pertain to many women who are not in the labor force. These women may be seriously disadvantaged in terms of educational attainment and potential occupational status. Second, these studies use scales of occupational status derived for men and use the scales to measure women's status as well as men's. Use of such scales has been severely criticized.[53]

In light of these shortcomings, it is not surprising that in spite of the apparent equality between the sexes in terms of educational and occupational attainment, women's *income* returns to education and occupational status are much lower than men's, even after controlling for work experience and hours worked per year.[54] Treiman and Terrell (1975) concluded that working married women are not able to convert educational attainment into earnings as effectively as their spouses and that they are paid less for doing work of comparable status.

Human Capital Theory. While status attainment theory was initially concerned with the relative effects of ascribed versus achieved characteristics, human capital theory has focused on returns to investments that presumably increase one's productivity. Educational attainment is used in human capital theory as a proxy for productivity. On-the-job training is also an important measure of productivity. Becker (1975) argues that on-the-job training is of two types: general training which increases the worker's marginal productivity in other firms as well as in the firm providing the training, and specific training which increases worker productivity more in the firm providing it than in other firms. While on-the-job training is rarely measured in national surveys, human capital theorists have used total work experience and tenure in current job as proxy variables.

Economists in the human capital tradition assume that the "traditional" division of household labor is economically rational. According to this rational choice model, family members specialize in either market work or household work in order to maximize household utility. Becker argues that women are biologically committed to bearing and rearing children, and hence are more efficient than men at household than at market work.[55] Furthermore, women sometimes provide support services for their spouses' careers.[56] This specialization leads women to make fewer investments than men in market capital, resulting in the "traditional" division of household labor.

According to human capital theory, women's anticipated and actual household responsibilities affect choice of occupation, work commitment, amount and continuity of labor force experience, hours of work, job training, etc.[57] Married women, especially those who have young children, may "attempt to maximize job benefits other than earnings," such as working hours and job location, to minimize interference with family responsibilities.[58] While men are assumed to maximize income from market work to provide for their families, human capital theory assumes that most women expect to invest more time in household than in market work.[59] As a result, young women seek less demanding jobs than men. In particular, they seek occupations and jobs that will allow them to move easily in and out of the labor force to accommodate the demands of child rearing. According to this human capital view, women choose to be secondary or marginal workers in order to give priority to their household work during marriage. Women emphasize market work before marriage, or in the event a marriage ends; after marriage or remarriage, women emphasize household work.

According to human capital theory, having children interferes with the accumulation of human capital by women. As a result, married women's market wages vary with number of children—the more children, the lower their wages.[60] Becker claims this variation is the result of two processes. Women who earn high wages find having more children increasingly costly, and women who have children invest more time in household skills and less in market skills. Researchers have found empirical support for both arguments. Haggstrom et al. (1984) found that women who earn high wages are less likely to have children. Mincer and Polachek (1974), using data from the 1967 National Longitudinal Survey of Women aged 30–44, found that the more children a woman has, the less work experience she is likely to have.

Women who have continuous work histories fare better than those who have frequent or lengthy interruptions for child rearing. Mincer and Polachek also argue that time spent out of the labor force for child rearing results in a depreciation of earning power.[61] Polachek (1975), extending the earlier analysis, found that discontinuity of work experience had a negative effect on wage rates of married women, even after controlling for amount of experience. However, the finding that women's earning power depreciates during periods of nonparticipation in the labor force has been controversial.[62]

Family Roles. Sociologists have sought to improve the explanatory power of the status attainment and human capital models by explicitly including measures of women's family roles. It is argued that family role variables have an indirect effect on wages (through their effects on levels of investment in human capital), as well as an independent direct effect.[63] The emphasis has been on the latter claim, i.e., that variables such as the presence and number of children at home have a direct effect, after controlling for human capital variables.

According to the family labor supply model, the family is an economic unit in which one spouse's labor market behavior affects the other's employment experience.[64] Schwartz (1979) has considered the reciprocal effects of spouses' earnings, wages, and hours worked. Husbands' and wives' earnings are positively correlated when both work. Women whose spouses have relatively high earnings are likely to have high wages. This relationship may be due to marital selection (women who have high earning power marry men who have high earning power), and/or to a higher "asking" (or "reservation") wage for women married to men who have high earnings (i.e., they work only if they find a job with relatively high wages). Hours worked by her spouse are not related to a woman's hours or earnings. However, a woman's hours worked are negatively correlated with her spouse's earnings, indicating that women work more if their spouses' incomes are low.

Children may also affect women's work outcomes. Cramer (1980) found a short-run decline in women's employment as a result of the birth of a child. This decline may be attributable to the child's young age, since mothers tend to return to work as the child approaches school age. Waite et al. (1985) found that women's labor force participation rate declines as a first birth approaches, and increases gradually after the birth, but not to previous levels. Many mothers who return to the labor force after the birth work part-time rather than full-time. These findings suggest that a married woman's employment depends not only on her own human capital, but also on the presence and ages of children and on her spouse's earnings.

A woman's attitudes toward work and family roles may also influence her work outcomes. Gender attitudes may reflect an orientation to the work place whose effects are too subtle to be detected by traditional human capital variables. Waite (1978) found that egalitarian gender attitudes are associated with somewhat higher current and anticipated labor force participation rates. Other studies[65] report that egalitarian attitudes have a statistically significant effect on subsequent labor force participation by married women. Coverman (1983) found that egalitarian gender attitudes had a positive effect on women's wages, even after controlling for other family role, human capital, and labor market segmentation variables.

Summary. The individualist model that is employed in this study incorporates elements of status attainment theory, human capital theory, and the extension of these theories to include the independent effects of family role measures. The human capital measures employed here are: years of education, years of work experience, tenure in current job, and whether the respondent received occupational training. Each of these measures is assumed to reflect a worker's productivity, or value to the firm. Occupational status, as measured by Bose scores, is the only status attainment measure employed. Bose scores are more appropriate measures of women's occupational status than are Duncan scores (see discussion in Appendix A). Several family role variables are considered for inclusion in the model. Annual earnings of other household members, presence of children, number of children, and egalitarian gender attitudes are all presumed to reflect women's incentives or disincentives for investing time in market work versus household labor.

1.5   MODELS OF WOMEN'S LABOR MARKET OUTCOMES: LABOR MARKET SEGMENTATION APPROACHES

The second major theory explaining work outcomes focuses on the influence of labor market structures. While there are several variants of this approach, they share the common assumption that the labor market is segmented and that demand for labor is heterogeneous. How the labor market is segmented is a matter of some debate, as is the selection of measures of segmentation. It has been argued that the labor market is segmented by structural variables: industry sector,[66] firm,[67] occupation[68] and/or internal versus external labor markets.[69] Hodson (1984) has argued that economic segmentation occurs at several levels, all of which must be considered.

The dominant segmentation theory has been drawn from dual economy theory, which asserts that there are two types of industries: a core (or monopoly) sector and a periphery (or competitive) sector. The former industries are capital-intensive, highly technological, highly concentrated, and highly profitable, while the latter are poorly capitalized, labor intensive, unconcentrated, and marginally profitable.[70] The primary labor market is characterized by large firms with "well-developed internal labor markets with established channels for advancement and predictable work rules."[71] Seniority provisions, rather than productivity or performance on the job, account for wage variation and for the relationship between years of experience and wages.[72] Wages are relatively high, employment is stable, and on-the-job training is important. The secondary labor market, on the other hand, is dominated by low-skill jobs in smaller firms with short career ladders, low wages, and employment instability. Workers are allocated to the primary and secondary labor markets on the basis of superficial characteristics such as age, race, and sex.[73] While the core sector tends to be dominated by large firms, primary-type jobs, and older white male workers, the periphery is dominated by small firms, secondary-type jobs, and black, female, and younger workers. These are not, however, deterministic relationships, but probabilistic ones.[74]

While segmentation theories originally focused on the difference in individual outcomes between the core and periphery *sectors*, recent attention has focused on the *firm*, for a variety of reasons. Decisions on hiring, job assignment, and promotion are made within firms.[75] Firm size may be a better measure of market power than the core–periphery distinction, since some small firms are located in the core sector and some large firms in the periphery sector. Firm size is associated with other dimensions of organizational structure that are important for determining individual earnings; these dimensions include, for example, the degree of standardization and documentation, the presence of internal labor markets, and the number of job levels in an internal labor market.[76] Attention has focused both on the effects of structural differences among firms (principally size) and on the effects of the internal structure of firms (mobility processes). The analysis of firms is viewed as especially important because it has the potential to link studies of organizational structure with studies of attainment processes.[77]

Before reviewing empirical studies of structural models of women's labor market outcomes, it is useful to summarize the variables (and their units of analysis) that have been hypothesized as parts of the structural model. At the most fundamental level, characteristics of jobs determine individual earnings.[78] Among the important characteristics of jobs are skill level for entry, importance of on-the-job training, availability of a promotion ladder, "length" of promotion ladder, decision latitude, supervisory status, job security, standardization of work rules, and age distribution within the job. Some or all of these characteristics are at least partially determined by the internal organization of the firm (e.g. whether there is an internal labor market). The internal organization of a firm is in turn at least partially determined by its structural position vis-à-vis other firms (e.g., firm size, market position), which in turn is at least partially determined by its industry sector (e.g., core versus periphery). It is also important to remember that the structural model does not claim that individual characteristics have no effect on work outcomes, but rather that their effects are constrained by labor market segmentation. The structural model includes both individual characteristics and labor market segmentation variables. While there are a variety of views on how individual characteristics and segmentation variables combine to produce labor market outcomes, the two sets of variables will be combined in this study using a simple assumption, which will be discussed in Chapter 4.[79] The following sections, therefore, review research on the influence of labor market segmentation on work outcomes.

   Job Characteristics. Studies of job characteristics have found that the levels of authority and responsibility associated with jobs affect earnings. Roos (1981) used two measures of authority relations in the work place: control (whether or not a worker has a boss or supervisor) and authority (the number of levels of subordinates below him/her—none, one, two or more). Roos found that women tended to have less control and authority than did men. Women also earned less than men who had the same amount of control and authority, even after controlling for age, education, hours worked per week, industry, and other occupational characteristics (e.g., prestige, percent female). Robinson and Kelley (1979) also found sex differences in the distributions of, and income returns to, control and authority. They argue that differences in monetary return for the same jobs are more important than differences in distribution of control in accounting for the male–female earnings gap. Robinson and Kelley speculate that the lower returns may be due to the lower profitability of the firms in which women have control (suggesting that firm or industry is important), the lower importance of women's supervisory positions (suggesting a need for further refinement of the measure), or the smaller size of the firms in which women have control (suggesting again that firm characteristics are important).

   Unionization is one of the most obvious forms of segmentation in the labor market. It represents an attempt to limit access to entry-level jobs and to create rules for advancement in the work place. Union jobs pay higher salaries than nonunion jobs, on average. Men are more likely to have union jobs than women,[80] primarily because they are more likely to have blue-collar jobs. Coverman (1983) found a significant positive effect of union membership on women's earnings (controlling for human capital, family role, and other segmentation variables).[81] In fact, union membership had a stronger effect on women's earnings than on men's earnings in her study. Freeman and Medoff (1984), in a review of several studies, conclude that union membership has a positive effect on wages of both men and women (although the effect may be slightly stronger for men).[82]

Baron and Bielby (1980)[83] have argued that internal labor markets may function so as to produce job segregation within firms that may account for wage inequality between men and women. Studies of individual firms provide evidence of crowding of women into low-ranking jobs with fewer responsibilities. Malkiel and Malkiel (1973) found that in one large firm, female professionals were paid about two-thirds the salary of male professionals, on average. While about half of this difference was due to the lower human capital of women, they found that men and women who had similar amounts of human capital were assigned to job levels in such a way as to disadvantage women. Halaby's (1979) analysis of data from one firm found that only 22% of the male–female salary gap could be accounted for by human capital differences, while 78% could be attributed to sex segregation by job (44%) and by rank (34%). He suggests that job segregation may indicate hiring discrimination, while rank segregation may indicate promotion discrimination.

Firm size. Studies of firm characteristics have focused primarily on the importance of firm size in determining earnings. Large firms pay workers more, perhaps because these firms are more profitable[84] and/or can better capitalize on workers' education.[85] Bibb and Form (1977) found that firm size is the most important determinant of women's earnings (especially for unskilled and service workers). Furthermore, large firms pay female workers higher salaries than small firms,[86] even in the periphery sector,[87] and are less sex-segregated than small firms.[88] Hodson (1984) found that plant size is a more important determinant of earnings for women than it is for men. He argues that large plants, by virtue of being more bureaucratized, may be less able to exercise informal discrimination against women.

Industry Sector. Beck et al. (1978) have used a measure of core versus periphery sector to account for gender inequality in earnings.[89] Using National Opinion Research Center (NORC) General Social Survey Data from 1975 and 1976, they found that 47% of workers in the periphery sector were female, compared with 36% in the core sector.[90] They also found significant negative effects of being female on earnings in the core sector, which they suggest constitutes sex discrimination. In the periphery sector, they did not find a significant negative effect of being female; women do share with men, however, the earnings disadvantage of being employed in this sector.[91] Beck et al. (1980), in a replication of their analysis, found that women are more likely to be in the periphery sector than men (70% vs. 44% in the 1976 Current Population Survey), and that women encounter stronger discrimination in the core sector. The combination of these factors, they argue, is an important cause of gender inequality in earnings.

Summary. Structural models do not measure demand (i.e., preferences for particular types of employees) directly.[92] Rather, other variables are used as proxies for demand, because they reflect the ability of employers to "buy" (offer a high enough wage to attract and keep) workers who have the preferred characteristics. Demand is reflected in wage differences among labor market segments. Following Hodson's (1984) argument, several levels of economic segmentation will be considered: job characteristics (jobs with certain characteristics pay higher salaries than others), firm size (large firms tend to pay higher salaries than small firms), and industry sector (firms in core industries pay higher salaries than firms in periphery industries).

The job characteristics considered here are union status, decision latitude, supervisory status, and job insecurity. In addition, measures of firm size and core versus periphery industry will be employed in the segmentation models. While these variables will be referred to as the segmentation *variables,* the structural *model* includes a combination of both segmentation variables and individual characteristics, as explained above. Each of the segmentation variables measures the extent to which a job is insulated from or subject to external market forces, which is the underlying dimension presumed to distinguish primary jobs from secondary jobs. Union jobs, jobs with high decision latitude, supervisory jobs, and jobs rated as relatively secure are primary-type jobs insofar as they are likely to have predictable work rules, opportunity for advancement, low turnover, require firm-specific skills, and are insulated from competition from workers outside the firm. Primary jobs are more likely to be found in large firms and core industries than in small firms and periphery industries.

1.6   OVERVIEW OF THE STUDY

This book employs both individualist and structural models of labor market outcomes to account for differences between divorced and married women. While divorce is a common event in the United States, it is nevertheless economically disruptive. This study contributes in several ways to an understanding of women's economic well-being and work behavior after divorce. First, it provides a *long-term* evaluation of the effects of divorce. Long-term outcomes reflect the impact of the adjustments women make in response to the immediate short-term drop in their standard of living. Second, this study compares the work outcomes of divorced women to those of once-married women and never-married women. This comparison provides insight into how marital history is related to work outcomes.[93] Explanatory models are developed to explain this relationship, and, at a more general level, to understand the linkages between work and family. Finally, this study views the effects of divorce in the context of the life course. The economic well-being of divorced women depends on their work history and family situation. While divorce is a disruptive life event, some women are better prepared for it than others.

The basic premises of this study are:

(1) Divorced women, on average, have a lower standard of living than married women.

(2) Women who have a stronger attachment to the labor market during marriage have a higher standard of living after divorce than women who have a weak attachment to the labor market. While this premise is hardly surprising, it focuses attention on variation in economic well-being after divorce, rather than on the average effects of divorce on economic well-being.

(3) Divorced women, on average, fare better in the labor market than married women. Because of economic need, divorced women work more hours and earn more than married women. These effects accumulate over time as women make adjustments in their work careers. These effects are difficult to detect in cross-sectional or short-term longitudinal studies, but can be identified in a long-term evaluation of the effects of divorce.

While the first and third premises may seem somewhat inconsistent, they refer to different measures of income. The former refers to family income and the latter refers to personal income. In spite of their higher personal income, women have a lower family income after divorce. While most prior studies focus primarily on the decline in family income, this study also focuses attention on the long-term effects of divorce on work outcomes.

Both individualist and structural models of labor market outcomes are employed to account for differences between divorced and married women. The individualist model is expected to account for a substantial portion of the labor market advantage of divorced women over married women, because it is presumed that this advantage reflects average differences between the two groups in the economic incentives to work. Segmentation variables are expected to account for very little of the labor market advantage of divorced women, because it is presumed that firms, for the most part, do not discriminate among women on the basis of marital status. However, it will be of interest to see how well the structural and individualist models perform in accounting for variation in labor supply, earnings, and wages.

This study develops a model of the long-term effects of divorce on economic well-being based on the life-course method. The effects of divorce are expected to vary depending on women's life cycle patterns of work and family roles before divorce. A simple typology of life cycle patterns is adapted from Lopata and Norr (1980). The traditional homemaker (a declining pattern among younger women) adopts, more or less permanently, the role of housewife. Intermittent workers interrupt their employment to raise children, and return to work when the children attend school or leave the household. The career woman is engaged in continuous full-time employment while attaining increasingly higher status positions over the course of her career. She is less likely to have children than other married women; if she has children, she interrupts her employment briefly, if at all. The impact of divorce on a woman's economic well-being depends on her prior work and family history. Homemakers who return to full-time employment due to marital disruption often have difficulty finding jobs to support themselves and their children, while career women are generally in a much better economic position after divorce. The economic well-being of intermittent workers is expected to fall somewhere in between. This life-course method places more emphasis on variation in the effects of divorce than do most previous approaches to the study of divorce.

To provide a comprehensive view of the economic effects of divorce, this book is organized around analyses of labor market outcomes and economic well-being. Chapter 2 reviews data and measurement issues and describes the measure of marital history to be used. Chapter 3 provides an overview of the average effects of divorce on economic well-being and work outcomes. Chapter 4 considers explanatory models of the effects of divorce on labor supply, while Chapter 5 focuses on personal income. In Chapter 6, a model is developed to account for variations in economic well-being among divorced women. Finally Chapter 7 returns to the questions and issues raised in this chapter and addresses them in light of the findings from the analytic chapters.

CHAPTER 2

Data and Measurement Issues

2.1 THE NATIONAL LONGITUDINAL SURVEYS OF MATURE WOMEN

This study utilizes data from the National Longitudinal Surveys of Mature Women (NLS) during the period 1967 to 1977. The NLS data set has several assets which make it appropriate for this analysis. It provides longitudinal data on marital status change among women, and it is national in scope. A major weakness of many previous studies is their attempt to measure the effects of divorce using cross-sectional data. A few longitudinal studies focused primarily on short-term outcomes, while the NLS data allow for the measurement of change in marital status and its effects over a 10-year period. In addition, while there are longitudinal data sets based on samples from particular states,[1] the applicability of findings based on such samples to the U.S. population as a whole is unknown.

The Panel Study of Income Dynamics (PSID) might also have been appropriate for this study. The PSID includes men and women of all ages, while the NLS sample chosen here includes only women aged 30 through 44 in 1967. The NLS has more detailed work experience measures for women than does the PSID. Except for 1976, data on married women's work experience in the PSID is based on their spouses' responses. Although the age limitations of the NLS sample may be viewed as restricting the applicability of findings to similarly aged women, a compensating advantage is that age variation in the effects of marital status change is less likely to complicate results.[2] For these reasons, the NLS was chosen over the PSID.

The use of data from waves of the NLS which became available after this research was begun would have provided measures of even longer-range outcomes (12 or 13 years versus 10 years). However, the price of using this new data is the further loss of cases due to attrition. Since a ten-year span seems sufficient to evaluate long-term outcomes, data from later waves were not incorporated. The data from the NLS cohort of mature women during the period 1967 to 1977 were, on balance, the best available for this study.

The National Longitudinal Surveys were designed by the Center for Human Resource Research at Ohio State University, under contract to the U.S. Department of Labor. Sampling and interviewing for the surveys were handled by the U.S. Bureau of the Census using procedures and concepts similar to those of the Current Population Survey. The NLS sample of women was selected to be representative of the 1967 civilian noninstitutionalized population of women aged 30 through 44 in the United States. Households in areas with large numbers of black residents were selected at a rate between 3 and 4 times higher than households in other areas, in order to create a sample of blacks large enough for reliable estimates of their characteristics. This design yielded a sample of 5,083 women, including 3,606 whites, 1,390 blacks, and 87 "other" (e.g., Asian, Native American) women, representing the nearly 18 million women aged 30 through 44 in 1967 in the U.S. civilian noninstitutional population. Further details of the sample design and fieldwork are available in Parnes et al. (1976) and Center for Human Resource Research (1981).

2.2 SAMPLE ATTRITION, 1967–1977

One problem common to all longitudinal studies is attrition of sample members. The original NLS cohort of 5,083 women was interviewed at home in 1967, 1969, 1971, 1972, and 1977, interviewed by telephone in 1974 and 1976, and by mail in 1968. By 1977, 3,964 women remained in the sample, representing a retention rate of 78% after ten years of the study. While some of the attrition was "natural" (e.g., the respondent had died, emigrated, or been institutionalized), other respondents refused to be interviewed in subsequent years, or could not be located. If respondents lost from the sample differ in important ways from those retained, results based on the 1977 sample could be biased, since the sample would no longer be representative.

Two studies of the NLS concluded that sample attrition was not a serious problem. An analysis of the 1972 data indicated that attrition was unlikely to bias the results seriously.[3] However, there were minor differences in retention rates in 1972 with respect to marital status and region of residence. An updated study of attrition rates after ten years concluded "the noninterviews had not seriously distorted the representativeness of the sample."[4]

While these findings are reassuring, they provide information on differences between lost and retained respondents only with respect to some of the variables of interest in this study. Therefore, a more comprehensive analysis of differences between respondents lost and retained after ten years was conducted. In the first step of this process the lost and retained cases were compared with respect to their means on the 1967 measures of the dependent and independent variables. While multivariate analyses of variance indicate that there are statistically significant differences between lost and retained cases with respect to the means of both dependent and independent variables, these differences are relatively minor. Cases lost from the sample fared slightly better than cases retained in the sample on the 1967 outcome measures used in this study. Specifically, women lost from the sample worked more hours, were less likely to be poor, and had higher wages and earnings in 1967 than women retained in the sample. Among the independent variables, women lost from the sample were less likely to have children (74% vs. 83%) and slightly more likely to be nonwhite (31% vs. 28%) than women retained in the sample. There is also a statistically significant difference between lost and retained cases in terms of their marital status distribution (see Table 2-1). Women retained in the sample until 1977 are slightly less likely to have been divorced, separated, never married, remarried, or widowed in 1967. To the extent that women lost from each of these categories are unlike women retained in them, results presented in this study may be biased; however, the differences in retention rates among women in different marital status categories are relatively minor, and any such bias is likely to be minimal.

Because the differences in means of lost and retained cases raise some

TABLE 2–1:
Distribution of Marital Status for Lost and Retained Cases, 1967

Marital Status	Retained Cases	Lost Cases	Retention Rate	(Number)
Married once	70.1%	64.2%	79.4%	(3,495)
Divorced	4.4	6.9	70.0	(253)
Separated	5.4	6.2	75.7	(285)
Never married	5.4	6.6	74.4	(290)
Remarried	11.9	12.7	76.9	(615)
Widowed	2.7	3.5	73.1	(145)
Total	100.0%[a]	100.0%[a]	78.0%	
(Number)	(3,964)	(1,119)		(5,083)
		Chi-square = 19.62**		

[a] Percentages do not total exactly 100% due to rounding.
** p < .01

questions concerning the representativeness of the sample, a second type of comparison of these cases was made. Two correlation matrices of all dependent and independent variables were created—one for lost cases and one for retained cases. Fisher's z-transformation was used to test for the significance of differences between correlations of lost and retained cases. The number of significant differences (at the .05 level) is no more than would be expected by chance. This finding suggests that while there are some differences in means between these two categories, the underlying correlational structure is the same. Results based on correlation matrices for retained cases are expected to be similar to those that would have been obtained had no cases been lost from the sample. Of course, this conclusion is based only on evidence from the 1967 data. There is no way of determining whether the correlational structure of variables for cases lost from the sample differed from that for retained cases in 1977.

2.3   DESCRIPTION OF MEASURES EMPLOYED IN THE STUDY

The two criteria by which any indicator is judged are validity (does the indicator measure what it is said to measure) and reliability (does the indicator provide consistent results over repeated measurements). In discussing the indicators in this chapter and in Appendix A, the emphasis is on establishment of face validity for the measures. Do the indicators, as constructed, appear to measure what they are claimed to measure? Evidence on reliability is also presented for those few variables for which it is available. Construct validity (the relationship of the indicator to other indicators in a way consistent with theoretically derived hypotheses[5]) will be established in later chapters.

Measuring Marital History. A weakness of most previous studies of the effects of divorce is their failure to adequately measure the concept of marital status. Many studies reviewed in Chapter 1 treated marital status as a static concept. It is argued here that women's socioeconomic characteristics are affected by changes in marital status over the life course (i.e., by marital history), not just by current marital status. As argued in Chapter 1, the economic situation of married women in their first marriage may be quite different from that of women who have remarried after divorce, and from women who have remarried after being widowed. While a few studies have made some of these distinctions, none has gone into sufficient detail in considering the effects of marital history.

A valid measure of marital status, for the purposes of this study, ought to include information about current marital status and about marital history (e.g., number of marriages, whether the respondent was ever divorced or widowed, and for how long). In the NLS, information about "current marital status" is available over several points in time. Additional data are available for 1967 and 1977: how many times the respondent has been married, when she was married, whether the marriage(s) ended, how the marriage(s) ended (widowed or divorced), and when the marriage(s) ended. However, the availability of this detailed information presents problems: How can such information be usefully summarized to create theoretically interesting categories? How many categories should be created? Given the limits of sample size in the NLS, how can small categories be combined without creating categories that are too heterogeneous?

This study is not concerned with the effects of widowhood, since the psychological and economic impact of widowhood may be very different from that of divorce.[6] For that reason, women who have ever been widowed are included in a miscellaneous "other" marital history category.

Leaving out women who have ever been widowed, marital history categories can be derived by cross-tabulating marital status (never married, married once, separated, divorced, remarried) in 1967 by marital status in 1977, creating nineteen logically possible categories.[7] This cross-tabulation creates too many categories, some of which are in any case theoretically uninteresting by themselves. Furthermore, some cell sizes are too small for reliable analysis, and some useful information from the five intermediate surveys is left out. To correct these shortcomings, more inclusive marital history categories are created by combining cells into theoretically interesting and relatively homogeneous categories. Information from intermediate surveys is used as a check on the accuracy of the 1977 measure of marital status (e.g., some women who answered "never married" in 1977 seem to have indicated in one or more of the intermediate surveys that they were married). Cases with such inaccurate or inconsistent information were generally placed in the miscellaneous "other" category (see exceptions discussed below). To deal with small cell sizes, some cells are combined to create larger categories. Other cells are dropped from the detailed analysis (e.g., women who were never married in 1967 but married, separated, divorced, or remarried in 1977[8]), and combined into the "other" category. Some measures cannot be used conveniently in defining the categories (e.g., years since divorce), but can be used as variables in the analysis. The marital history categories, the conditions a case must fulfill to be placed in each of the categories, and the total number of cases in each category are presented in tabular form (see Table 2-2).

Note that the women in the recently divorced and recently separated categories are not necessarily divorced or separated from their 1967 spouse. It is possible that they divorced and remarried in the intervening survey years. Similarly, long-term divorced women and long-term separated women may have experienced one or more remarriages ending in divorce or

TABLE 2–2: *Description of Marital History Categories*

Category	Number
1. Married throughout: Married only once in 1967 and 1977, marital status in all intervening surveys reported as "currently married" or as "missing."	2,273
2. Recently divorced: Married in 1967, divorced in 1977.	172
3. Long-term divorced: Divorced in 1967 and 1977.	170
4. Never married: Never married in 1967 and 1977, marital status in all intervening surveys reported as "never married" or as "missing."	164
5. Recently separated: Married in 1967, separated in 1977.	101
6. Long-term separated: Separated in 1967 and 1977	84
7. Remarried throughout: Married two or more times in both 1967 and 1977; no divorces or new marriages reported in intervening survey years.	267
8. Remarried, divorced after 1967: Married once in 1967, married twice or more in 1977.	81
9. Remarried, divorced in 1967: Divorced in 1967, remarried by 1977.	76
10. Other: Includes women widowed from last marriage; remarried widows; women who married for the first time between 1967 and 1977; once-married women who separated from their spouse between 1967 and 1977 and who reported themselves as married to the same spouse in 1977 as 1967; women whose responses to marital history questions were inconsistent (e.g., reported as never married in 1977, yet as married in one of the previous survey years); and all women not included in any of the above categories.	572
Total, all categories[a]	3,960

[a] Four cases are not included here since their 1977 marital status was reported as missing.

separation between 1967 and 1977. Women who remarried after 1967 may have been divorced and remarried several times between 1967 and 1977.[9] Women in these categories who experienced such remarriages were *not* taken out of their categories and placed in the "other" category, for three reasons. First, the measures available to determine whether such remarriages occurred are unreliable. Data on number of marriages in 1967 and 1977 are sometimes inconsistent. For example, some women report fewer marriages in 1977 than in 1967. It is likely that some reports of more marriages in 1977 than in 1967 are also unreliable. Data from intervening surveys support this conclusion. Second, dropping cases from some of these categories would make categories too small for useful analysis. Third, where evidence of intervening remarriages was consistent, no meaningful differences between women who had experienced and those who had not experienced such remarriages could be detected on a variety of variables used in this study. In summary, given the need to maintain adequate category sizes, the possible unreliability of the measures of intervening remarriages, and the evidence that, where they appear to be reliably measured (i.e., all responses are consistent), women with intervening remarriages were no different from those without, it was decided not to drop such cases from these categories.

In concluding this discussion of the measurement of marital history, several comments are in order about separated women. Many short separations end in reconciliation;[10] where there was evidence of this, cases were placed in the "other" category. A few recently separated women might have reconciled with their spouses after 1977; such cases are unlikely to distort the results presented here. Other recently separated women may have divorced their spouses after 1977. Where appropriate, results for recently separated women will be interpreted in light of the possibility that these women may be in the process of divorcing.

The long-term separated women may seem to be an anomalous group. Some of these women may not have been separated throughout the ten years, as explained above. However, data on number of marriages and on marital status in intervening years indicate that, at most, 9 of the 84 women were married at some time between 1967 and 1977. Of the 84 women, 62 reported themselves as separated at all seven interviews from 1967 to 1977.[11] Some separated women may have been unwilling or unable to obtain a divorce for religious, legal, or financial reasons. Others may have misreported their marital status. A substantial proportion of long-term separated women receive public assistance payments. If some of the women receiving public assistance were actually married, and feared that their survey responses would be shared with public assistance agencies, they may have reported themselves as separated. This misreporting may also have occurred among recently separated women. Results for the two categories should be interpreted with these factors in mind.

Measuring Dependent and Independent Variables. A description of the measurement of dependent and independent variables is presented in Appendix A. Data on the distributions of these variables are presented in Appendix B and Appendix C. Note that some of the measures (e.g., annual hours, family income) pertain to 1966 and 1976 rather than 1967 and 1977, since these survey questions refer to the year prior to the year of the interview.

2.4 ANALYTIC ISSUES

Weighted versus Unweighted Results. Weights are available for each case in the NLS data set to adjust for differential probabilities of selection into the sample (most important, the oversampling of blacks) and for noninterviews in the initial sampling frame. Adjustments were also made so that the distribution of the sample conformed to the known distribution of the population (of U.S. women aged 30 through 44) with respect to race residence, and age in 1967. Weights were adjusted for nonrandom attrition in each of the subsequent surveys.[12] Weighting has a relatively minor impact on results using the 1977 data, with one exception—the proportion of blacks in the sample using weighted data is much lower (12%) than in the unweighted sample (28%). The use of the weights has an obvious effect on estimates based on certain other variables; for example, the unweighted poverty rate is 20%, while the weighted poverty rate is 15%. For most other variables the impact of weighting is not as dramatic.

Some researchers using the NLS have presented results separately by race, or presented results for whites only. Splitting the sample by racial groups would result in marital history category sizes too small for analysis (see section on "Measuring Marital History," above). Analyzing only whites would provide an inadequate picture of the effects of marital history. In this study, results are presented for the whole sample. While the oversampling was designed to allow more reliable estimates for blacks, a problem arises when results are desired for the whole sample: should one use weighted or unweighted results? The answer to that question depends on the purpose of the analysis and on the type of results being presented. If a statistic, such as a mean, is intended to describe the U.S. population, then it ought to be based on weighted data. However, when testing differences among the means of several groups, the significance tests ought to be based on the true (unweighted) number of cases, rather than the weighted number, since weighting reduces efficiency of the estimates in such situations. Regression analyses generally ought to ‾be conducted on unweighted data. If the assumptions of regression hold, every case represents an independent observation from the population; weighting, however, implies that some observations are more important than others, since a weighted regression line fits cases with higher weights better than cases with lower weights.

Since this study is primarily concerned with relationships between variables, and their statistical significance, unweighted results will be presented, unless otherwise indicated. Regression results, for the reasons described above, are always based on unweighted data.[13] In Chapter 3, which is concerned with both describing the population and testing relationships between variables, most results are presented for unweighted data. All tables were run using both weighted and unweighted data: in most cases, the differences are minor. Since significance tests for unweighted data are more efficient, unweighted data are presented. Only where results differ sharply are weighted results presented.

Significance Testing. In a large sample such as the NLS, there are likely to be variables whose distribution does not approximate a normal distribution because there are extreme observations, usually in the higher values of the distribution. Such "long upper tails" can drastically alter the mean and substantially increase the variance, thereby reducing the efficiency of statistical tests of significance.[14] The distributions of variables employed in this study were examined to determine whether they had long upper tails, using a procedure developed by Tukey.[15] An attempt was made to find a transformation (i.e., re-expression) of such variables so as to "pull in the tail" (i.e., make the distribution more nearly normal). Variables measured in hours and dollars (i.e., annual hours, hourly wages, annual earnings, annual family income) had long upper tails and were transformed using natural logarithms. Variables which were transformed using natural logarithms are followed in the Tables by the symbol "Ln" (e.g., Wage, 1977 (Ln)). Data on the skewness of variables before and after transformation are presented (see Appendix Table B-1).

The justification for working with transformed variables is a statistical one. Significance tests are more valid as the distributions of variables approach the normal distribution, since linear models generally have difficulty predicting outliers and other cases in long straggling tails of a distribution. Substantive conclusions drawn from the significance tests on transformed variables are more realistic. However, using transformed variables raises two issues—one theoretical and the other technical.

The theoretical issue concerns whether transforming a variable changes its meaning. In the sense that the scale of a transformed variable is different (i.e., the units are no longer the same), the meaning of the variable is changed. However, if what one is really interested in is measuring the relationship between that variable and other variables, then a transformation allows for the expression of the variables on a scale more suited for statistical tests. In some cases, but not all, the results using the transformed variable can be interpreted in a meaningful way. Regression coefficients predicting the natural logarithm of hourly wage, for example, approximate percentage (rather than absolute) changes in hourly wage.

The technical issue concerns how results using transformed variables ought to be presented. Several alternatives are available. One can simply present results using the transformed data. A second approach is to present results (e.g., means) using untransformed variables, but to perform statistical tests on the transformed variables. A third alternative is to use a linear transformation of the transformed variable so that the units of the transformed variable are roughly similar in magnitude to those of the original variable.[16] An attempt was made to find a linear transformation for the variables in this study, but finding a transformation that yields meaningful values over the whole distribution proved too difficult. In this study both the first and second alternatives are employed. In some cases (e.g., regression results), estimates for transformed data are presented along with their significance tests. In other cases (e.g., analyses of variance), estimates based on untransformed data are presented to provide interpretable results. Statistical tests are performed on the transformed data and presented in the same table.

Significance tests in Chapter 3 are the conventional two-tailed tests of analysis of variance. Significance tests in subsequent chapters (regression analyses) are one-tailed tests, unless otherwise indicated. Only where the direction of the effect has not been predicted are two-tailed tests employed.

Treatment Of Missing Data. For the most part, cases with missing data on a variable are dropped from any analysis using that variable. However, in some situations, mean-substitution is used; that is, the mean of the variable is assigned to cases with missing data. Mean-substitution is used in multiple regression equations for which one or two independent variables have considerably more missing data than the other independent variables. This procedure allows data from other variables to be used in the analysis of a case with data missing on one variable.[17] Instances where mean substitution is used are clearly indicated.

Further discussion of the details of the data analysis and their substantive implications is provided in the following chapters.

CHAPTER 3

Overview of the Economic Effects of Divorce

There is a considerable body of evidence indicating that women in the United States increase their labor supply after divorce, but suffer a sharp decline in economic well-being. Some of this research is cross-sectional,[1] while some uses short-term longitudinal data.[2] Weitzman (1985), for example, focuses on the economic problems of divorced women in the first year after divorce. Most studies consider only one or two dependent variables.[3] In this chapter, the economic changes accompanying divorce are described using a variety of measures, focusing on both short-term and long-term consequences.

Two kinds of evidence are considered here. *Panel data* are presented for women who have different marital histories. By examining changes for each of these groups from 1967 to 1977, one can determine how marriage and divorce affect women's work careers and economic well-being. Divorced women are compared to women who remained in their first marriage, whose work careers and economic situation represent the best estimate of what women's lives would be like in the absence of divorce. Furthermore, the long-term effects of divorce are considered by comparing two groups of divorced women—those divorced since 1967 and those divorced before 1967.[4]

The second kind of evidence presented here considers *time series* data for 217 women divorced between 1966[5] and 1977. In the time series data, a woman's year of divorce is considered to be year 0, the year after divorce is considered to be year $+1$, one year before divorce is considered to be year -1, etc. Not all women contributed data for each year in the time series, for three reasons. First, some women did not respond to particular survey questions. Second, interviews were not conducted in every year, so that each respondent has data available for some years but not others. As an example of this limitation, a woman who became divorced in 1974 has data available on labor force status for 1972 (year -2) and 1976 (year $+2$), but not for 1973 (year -1) or 1975 (year $+1$), when no NLS interviews were conducted. Third, women divorced toward the beginning or end of the 10-year period could not contribute as many years of data for the period before or after divorce. For example, a woman divorced in 1966 has no data available on earnings in the year before divorce, and a woman divorced in 1977 has no data available on labor force participation in the year after divorce.

The number of respondents who could contribute observations to the time series many years after or before divorce was small, therefore the time series data presented here are limited to 6 years before and after divorce. In each time series figure, a smooth curve was fit to the data points using linear, quadratic, and cubic terms. A cubic fit was chosen to allow for two bends in the slope of the line, allowing for both an acceleration and deceleration of the observed trend. In some figures only one bend appears within the range of data considered here.[6] This time series data enables one to determine whether changes pre-date the divorce, and to determine whether changes that occur in the first year or two after divorce persist several years later.

3.1 LABOR SUPPLY

As noted in Chapter 1, women's labor force participation increased substantially throughout the 1960s and 1970s.[7] In the NLS sample, the labor force participation rate increased from 52% to 60% between 1967 and 1977 (Table 3-1). The NLS reflects the experience of a particular cohort of women as they aged during the period 1967–1977; the data do not necessarily reflect the experience of the entire female labor force.[8]

A breakdown of changes in labor force participation rates by marital history categories indicates that recently divorced women showed the greatest increase, from 55% to 81% (Table 3-1). However, this 26 percentage point increase cannot be attributed entirely to divorce, since women who remained married throughout the period also showed a net percentage point increase, though not as large (13%). The net effect of divorce on labor force participation rates appears to be 13% (26%—13%).[9]

Women who were married in 1967 and divorced in 1977 ("recently divorced") already had a higher labor force participation rate than married women in 1967 (55% vs. 44%). This is also true of women who were married in 1967 and separated in 1977 ("recently separated"). Women who experience a marital disruption are more likely to have been working while married than other married women.[10] Some women may anticipate marital

TABLE 3–1:

Labor Force Participation Rates by Marital History, 1967 and 1977

Marital History	Participation Rates		(Number)
	1967	1977	
Married throughout	44%	57%	(2,273)
Recently divorced	55%	81%	(172)
Long-term divorced	81%	77%	(170)
Never married	74%	71%	(164)
Recently separated	52%	57%	(101)
Long-term separated	71%	63%	(84)
Remarried throughout	55%	57%	(267)
Remarried, divorced after 1967	53%	67%	(81)
Remarried, divorced in 1967	79%	57%	(76)
Other	60%	61%	(572)
Total, all cases	52%	60%	(3,960)

disruption by returning to the labor force while still married.[11] To the extent that it reflects anticipation of divorce, this difference in rates of labor force participation could also be considered an "effect" of divorce.[12]

While divorce has a positive effect on labor force participation rates, remarriage has a negative effect. The effects of remarriage can be evaluated by considering data from two of the marital history groups. Of women who were married in 1967 and divorced by 1977, those who remarried ("remarried, divorced after 1967") experienced an increase in labor force participation rates, although not as great an increase as for those who remained divorced ("recently divorced"). This comparison with divorced women suggests that remarriage reduces labor force participation rates. There is even stronger evidence of a reduction in labor force participation rates among those who were divorced in 1967 and remarried in 1977 ("remarried, divorced in 1967"). In 1967, their rate (79%) was similar to that of other divorced women ("long-term divorced"), while in 1977 their rate (57%) was similar to that of other married women ("married throughout").

Women who were single at both time points (long-term divorced or separated, or never married) generally had higher rates of labor force participation than married women in both 1967 and 1977 (although all three groups experienced some absolute decline over time). This finding supports the argument that single women have stronger incentives to work than married women.

A clearer picture of how divorce is associated with labor force participation can be seen in the time series analysis (see Figure 3-1). Labor force participation rates begin to rise as early as 4 years before divorce, increasing from 58% five years before divorce to 74% in the year of divorce. In the first and second year before divorce, many of these women were presumably already separated from their spouses. However, the increases which occur 3 or 4 years before divorce probably indicate that women seek employment in anticipation of separating from their spouses.[13] Labor force participation continues to increase after divorce (peaking above 80%), presumably in response to the economic need experienced by divorced women. Considered together, these findings suggest that some women anticipate marital disruption by returning to work, while for others, work is a response to the economic hardship following divorce.

Overall, women's annual hours worked increased by about 12% between 1967 and 1977, reflecting the same underlying trends discussed for labor force participation (see Table 3-2). Increases in women's labor supply are probably due in part to women's increasing real wages during this period. While men generally supply less labor as their wages increase, women generally supply more labor as their wages increase.[14] Thus the recent historical trend for men is a decline in labor supply, while women's labor

TABLE 3–2: *Mean Annual Hours by Marital History, 1966 and 1976*

Marital History	1966	Year (Number)	1976	(Number)
Married throughout	1,350	(1,088)	1,580	(1,259)
Recently divorced	1,360	(94)	1,820**	(131)
Long-term divorced	1,770***	(130)	1,800**	(123)
Never married	1,930***	(113)	1,890***	(112)
Recently separated	1,280	(62)	1,600	(55)
Long-term separated	1,440	(59)	1,420	(56)
Remarried throughout	1,440	(160)	1,490	(150)
Remarried, divorced after 1967	1,330	(53)	1,480	(52)
Remarried, divorced in 1967	1,660**	(63)	1,590	(47)
Other	1,460*	(338)	1,620	(321)
Total, all cases	1,440	(2,160)	1,610	(2,306)
	$eta^2 = .04$***		$eta^2 = .02$***	

NOTE: Significance tests were performed on transformed data (natural logarithm of hours worked) to correct for positive skewness (non-normality) in the raw data.
      Significance levels refer to differences between the group's mean and the mean for women "married throughout."
  * $p < .05$
 ** $p < .01$
*** $p < .001$

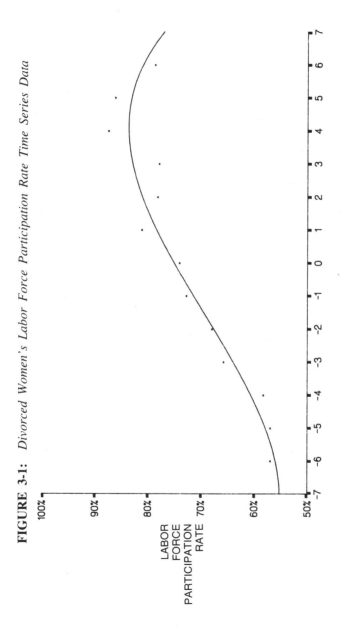

FIGURE 3-1: *Divorced Women's Labor Force Participation Rate Time Series Data*

supply is increasing, as real wages have risen. The size of this increase, however, suggests that some other factor, such as changing "tastes for work,"[15] is also increasing women's labor supply.

The analyses for annual hours (as well as for annual earnings and hourly wage in the next section) are restricted to working women. According to Heckman (1974), there is a "selection bias" in restricting analyses to working women. Women who do not work are those whose asking wage (measuring the value of their nonmarket time) is higher than their offered wage ("the wage a woman faces in the market"[16]). For women who do work, the offered wage is assumed to be greater than or equal to the asking wage. In this context, there are two explanations for why a woman is not working. Either her asking wage may be relatively high (holding offered wage constant), or the wage she is offered may be relatively low (holding asking wage constant). In any case, one cannot observe hours, wages, or earnings.

This selection bias may affect the analyses of data for working women presented in this chapter. The relationship between marital history and hours, earnings, or wages might be weaker than it appears. For example, characteristics of divorced women (other than their marital history) may increase their labor force participation rate *and* make them more likely to work longer hours or to have higher earnings or wages. Heckman proposed that analyses of hours, earnings or wages of working individuals should include a control for their probability of working, as a correction for selection bias. This correction will be employed in subsequent chapters. This chapter provides a description, rather than an explanation, of labor force characteristics, and therefore the results presented here do not control for selection bias.

The results for annual hours (presented in Table 3-2), can be summarized simply. In both 1966 and 1976, women who were divorced or never married worked more hours than continuously married or remarried women. Women's hours worked are quite responsive to both divorce and remarriage.[17] Separated women were the only "single" women who did not work more hours than married women. Separated women may be recent entrants to the labor market who have not yet found full-time work, or they may be women who do not have the education or training to obtain full-time work.

The time series data (Figure 3-2) indicate that annual hours begin to increase one year before divorce, a time when most of these women would have just separated from their spouses. Hours worked continue to increase until five years after divorce. Apparently, women anticipate marital disruption by increasing labor force participation before separation, but do not increase their hours of work until after the separation. After divorce, there is a clear increase in hours worked.

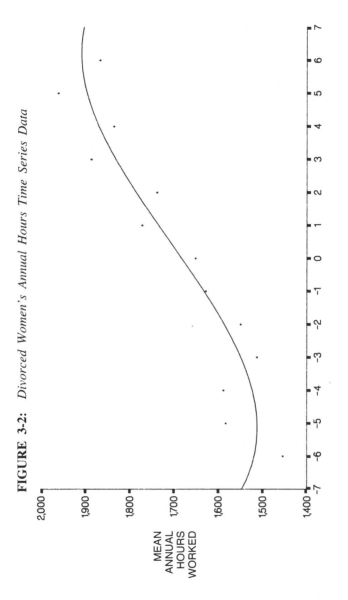

FIGURE 3-2: *Divorced Women's Annual Hours Time Series Data*

Several conclusions can be drawn concerning the relationship between marital status and labor supply: (1) Divorce increases labor supply while remarriage reduces labor supply. Recently divorced women were more likely than married women to enter the labor force and to work more hours. Women who were initially divorced in 1967 and who remarried by 1977 showed a decline in labor force participation rate and a slight decline in hours worked. (2) The effect of separation on labor supply appears to be minimal. (3) The labor supply of divorced women is much closer to that of never-married women than of married women. (4) Although remarriage reduces labor force participation rates, recently remarried women are more likely to work than continuously married women. This finding may indicate that some remarried women wish to remain able to support themselves in the event of another divorce.[18]

3.2 PERSONAL INCOME

The average earnings of working women increased by 38% in real dollars between 1966 and 1976 (see Table 3-3). In each year, currently married women (whether married one or more times) earn less than currently divorced and never-married women. Recently divorced women increased their earnings substantially, while women who remarried have earnings similar to women still married to the same spouse ("married throughout"). These patterns reflect those for annual hours, which is not surprising, since annual earnings depend in part on hours worked. Married women who were about to divorce in 1967 (i.e., the group referred to as "recently divorced" as of 1977) had slightly higher earnings than other married women in 1966. This finding is consistent with the hypothesis that married women who have greater earning power are more economically independent of their spouses and are therefore more likely to leave the marriage.[19]

Women recently separated in 1977 also increased their earnings; however their earnings when still married in 1966 had been lower than the earnings of women who would remain married through 1977, so that in spite of their increase, they did not earn much more than these married women in 1976. This increase appears, at least in part, to be due to the fact that fewer of them were working in 1976 than in 1966, and may reflect a polarization of these separated women into two categories. Those who continued to work were those who had higher earnings; those who stopped working were those who had lower earnings. Among long-term separated women, earnings were also low in 1966; however the earnings of these women did not keep pace with those of any other category of women over time. These findings indicate

TABLE 3–3:

Mean Annual Earnings by Marital History, 1966 and 1976
(1976 Dollars)

Marital History	Year 1966	(Number)	1976	(Number)	Percent Change in Real Earnings
Married throughout	$4,550	(1,024)	$6,130	(1,145)	+35%
Recently divorced	5,220	(97)	7,950***	(139)	+52%
Long-term divorced	5,950***	(136)	8,500***	(127)	+43%
Never married	7,330***	(113)	9,220***	(111)	+26%
Recently separated	3,430*	(64)	6,370	(54)	+86%
Long-term separated	3,520	(66)	4,180*	(56)	+19%
Remarried throughout	4,300	(153)	5,220	(147)	+21%
Remarried, divorced after 1967	3,760	(45)	6,000	(52)	+60%
Remarried, divorced in 1967	5,600***	(65)	6,840	(43)	+22%
Other	4,080	(345)	5,980	(304)	+46%
Total, all cases	$4,670	(2,108)	$6,430	(2,178)	+38%
	eta^2 = .03***		eta^2 = .03***		

NOTE: Significance tests were performed on transformed data (natural logarithm of earnings) to correct for positive skewness (non-normality) in the raw data.

Significance levels refer to differences between the group's mean and the mean for women "married throughout."

* p < .05
*** p < .001

that separated women are disadvantaged not only relative to married women, but also relative to divorced women.

The time series data (Figure 3-3) provide further elaboration of the relationship between divorce and earnings. The data show that real annual earnings of divorced women increased steadily in the years before divorce, as they did for all women over the survey period. However, there is a sharper increase in earnings in the years after divorce (with a temporary decline in years 3 and 4), presumably in response to economic need accompanying loss of spouse's income. The higher earnings of divorced women seem to represent an acceleration of a trend begun before the divorce.

The mean hourly real wage[20] of NLS women increased by 17% between 1967 and 1977 (see Table 3-4).[21] The real mean wage of long-term divorced women showed the largest increase (39%) of any marital history group over the ten years of the study. By 1977 their mean wage was significantly higher than that of married women. In contrast, the mean wage increase of women

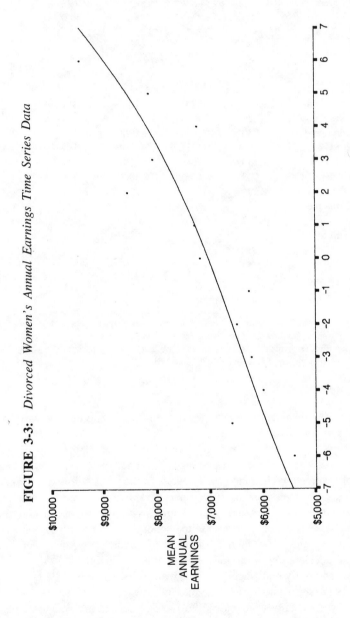

FIGURE 3-3: *Divorced Women's Annual Earnings Time Series Data*

TABLE 3–4:

Mean Hourly Wage at Current Job by Marital History, 1967 and 1977
(1977 Dollars)

Marital History	1967	(Number)	1977	(Number)	Percent Change in Real Wages
		Year			
Married throughout	$3.57	(808)	$4.01	(1,036)	+12%
Recently divorced	4.06*	(83)	4.39	(126)	+8%
Long-term divorced	3.49	(124)	4.86***	(117)	+39%
Never married	4.08	(98)	4.96***	(102)	+22%
Recently separated	2.95***	(46)	3.82	(49)	+29%
Long-term separated	2.68***	(52)	3.31***	(49)	+24%
Remarried throughout	3.37	(124)	3.62*	(123)	+7%
Remarried, divorced after 1967	3.73	(30)	3.89	(41)	+4%
Remarried, divorced in 1967	3.62	(55)	4.19	(39)	+16%
Other	2.98***	(295)	3.72**	(297)	+25%
Total, all cases	$3.46	(1,715)	$4.04	(1,979)	+17%
	$eta^2 = .04***$		$eta^2 = .02***$		

NOTE: Significance tests were performed on transformed data (natural logarithm of wage) to correct for positive skewness (non-normality) in the raw data.

Significance levels refer to differences between the group's mean and the mean for women "married throughout."

* $p < .05$
** $p < .01$
*** $p < .001$

recently divorced in 1977 did not keep pace with the increase among married women. Recently divorced women had significantly higher mean wages in 1967 than women who would remain married through 1977 ($4.06 vs. $3.57 per hour).[22] However, by 1977, their mean wage was not significantly higher than that of married women, because divorce caused more of them to enter the labor force than would otherwise have entered (as documented earlier). These recent entrants are women who were absent from the labor force for long periods of time and who, as a result, have lower earning power. This explanation is supported in a supplementary analysis (data not shown) restricted to women who worked in both 1967 and 1977: among this group, recently divorced women had significantly higher mean wages in 1977 than married women ($4.75 per hour vs. $4.42 per hour, respectively). The pattern of findings for the recently divorced and the long-term divorced suggests that while mean wages of divorced women are initially low because many are "pushed" into the labor market, over the long term, divorced women make adjustments to increase their earning power.

Women who were divorced in 1967 but who remarried are quite similar to women who remained in their first marriage. They experienced a 16% increase in mean wage. However, this increase may have occurred because many of these women (probably those who had low wages) dropped out of the labor force. In the other marital history categories, women separated before 1967 had significantly lower wages than married women in both years. Women who would be separated after 1967 had lower wages than other married women in 1967. The fact that women separated after 1967 had lower wages than women divorced after 1967 may reflect differences in the degree to which women who experience marital dissolution can afford a divorce. The wages of never-married women were only slightly higher than those of married women in 1967, but by 1977 were significantly higher.

The time series data (Figure 3-4) provide a mixed picture of the effect of divorce on wages. There is a generally increasing trend in wages through the year after divorce, followed by a decrease in mean wages in the next three years, and then a generally increasing trend in wages after that. While this pattern might represent random fluctuation, a plausible explanation is that the decline in wages after divorce may reflect the movement of new entrants into the labor market at low wages. If so, this pattern supports the earlier speculation that divorce results in an initial drop in mean wages, followed by' a significant increase, because divorced women make work adjustments to eventually increase their earning power.

3.3 ECONOMIC WELL-BEING

It was argued earlier that the increase in women's labor supply, annual earnings, and hourly wages after divorce is due to an increase in economic need associated with the loss of spouse's income. This section considers how economic need changes after divorce, specifically whether the economic situation of divorced women improves over time. Several types of data are presented: family income, income/needs ratio, poverty rates, and public assistance status.

The data on family income (Table 3-5) show a clear and consistent advantage for married women, as expected, due to the contribution of spouse's earnings. In both 1966 and 1976, women who were currently married (whether once or more) had higher mean family income than women who were not currently married (whether divorced, separated, or never married). Looking at changes over time, becoming divorced or separated

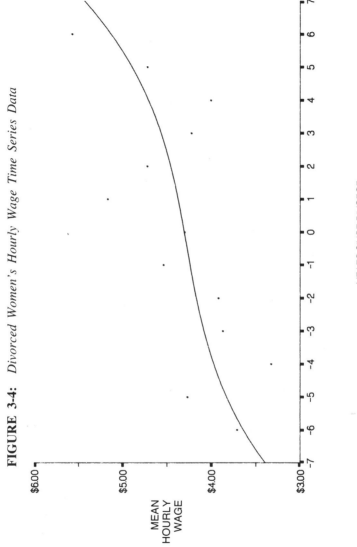

FIGURE 3-4: *Divorced Women's Hourly Wage Time Series Data*

TABLE 3–5:

Mean Family Income by Marital History, 1966 and 1976
(1976 Dollars)

Marital History	1966	(Number)	1976	(Number)	Percent Change in Real Family Income
Married throughout	$15,350	(2,249)	$19,260	(2,087)	+25%
Recently divorced	15,220	(171)	9,750***	(162)	−36%
Long-term divorced	7,960***	(167)	9,080***	(165)	+14%
Never married	8,280**	(157)	8,440***	(157)	+2%
Recently separated	11,480**	(99)	6,040***	(96)	−47%
Long-term separated	4,900***	(84)	4,890***	(80)	—
Remarried throughout	14,090	(263)	17,060	(250)	+21%
Remarried, divorced after 1967	14,190	(79)	17,950	(73)	+26%
Remarried, divorced in 1967	7,660*	(74)	14,380*	(70)	+88%
Other	10,430**	(562)	10,680***	(527)	+2%
Total, all cases	$13,460	(3,905)	$15,760	(3,667)	+17%
	eta^2 = .01*		eta^2 = .05***		

NOTE: Significance tests were performed on transformed data (natural logarithm of income) to correct for positive skewness (non-normality) in the raw data.

Significance levels refer to differences between the group's mean and the mean for women "married throughout."

* p < .05
** p < .01
*** p < .001

after 1967 resulted in a significant decline in family income, while remarriage increased family income.[23]

Perhaps a more accurate measure of differences in economic well-being is the income/needs ratio, which takes into account differences in family size between married and unmarried women.[24] Married women generally live in larger families than unmarried women, and their families therefore need more income. While there is disagreement over how to define the minimum income required to meet basic economic needs, the Census definition of the poverty threshold is a standard, easily available measure. A measure of each family's standard of living was computed by dividing total family income by the poverty threshold for a given family size.

Time series data for the income/needs ratio are presented in Figure 3-5.

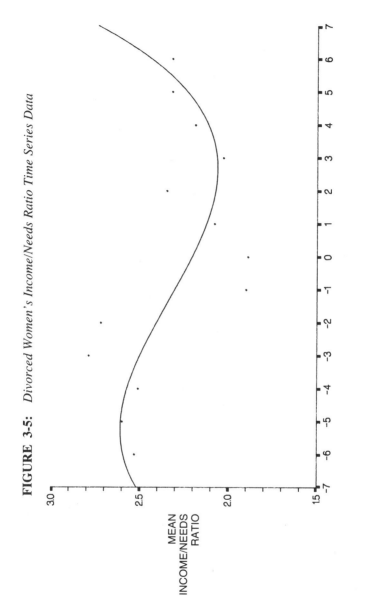

FIGURE 3-5: *Divorced Women's Income/Needs Ratio Time Series Data*

The mean standard of living drops sharply in the year before divorce, to about 70% of its level in the previous year. As noted earlier, this is a time when most of these women have just separated from their spouses. In the year after divorce, their standard of living begins to increase; by five or six years after divorce, the standard of living of divorced women is about 85% of what it had been before separation. These findings are consistent with those of other studies based on representative national samples. The sharpest drop in standard of living occurs immediately before divorce (i.e., at the time of separation), and is followed by a partial recovery in subsequent years.

While the income/needs ratio is a general measure of economic well-being, poverty status and public assistance status are measures that provide information about severe economic deprivation. Results for poverty status and for public assistance status are based on weighted data. Weighting is used only to present more realistic (that is, representative) results for these two variables. Differences between weighted and unweighted results are relatively minor in the data presented thus far; however, such differences are larger with respect to poverty status and public assistance status. For the most part, these differences are due to the oversampling of blacks (who are more likely than whites to be poor) in the stratified NLS. Nonwhites constitute 28% of the unweighted sample, but only 12% of the weighted sample.

Poverty rates were 25% and 20% in 1966 and 1976, respectively, without weighting, and 18% and 15% after weighting (Table 3-6). Weighted and unweighted results are quite similar with respect to differences among the marital history categories, since the distribution of race within marital

TABLE 3–6:   *Poverty Rates by Marital History, 1966 and 1976 (Weighted Percentages)*

Marital History	1966	Year (Number)	1976	(Number)
Married throughout	14%	(2,249)	12%	(2,087)
Recently divorced	17%	(171)	18%	(162)
Long-term divorced	35%	(167)	26%	(165)
Never married	22%	(157)	22%	(157)
Recently separated	28%	(99)	43%	(96)
Long-term separated	66%	(84)	60%	(80)
Remarried throughout	14%	(263)	10%	(250)
Remarried, divorced after 1967	20%	(79)	12%	(73)
Remarried, divorced in 1967	27%	(74)	17%	(70)
Other	27%	(562)	22%	(527)
Total, all cases	18%	(3,905)	15%	(3,667)

history categories is quite similar before and after weighting. Weighting does not "control" for race, it merely adjusts estimates so that they are nationally representative of the cohort of women aged 30 through 44 in 1967.

Women married to the same husband from 1967 to 1977 experienced a slight decline in poverty rate between 1966 and 1976, from 14% to 12% (Table 3-6). Surprisingly, becoming divorced during the survey period did not significantly increase a woman's chances of being in poverty.[25] Becoming separated, unlike becoming divorced, was associated with a large increase in poverty rate, from 28% to 43%. Long-term divorced women experienced a 9 percentage point decline in poverty rate. Nonetheless, over one-fourth remained poor in 1976. Remarriage, as would be expected, reduces poverty rates.

The time series data (Figure 3-6) present a more precise picture of the effect of divorce on the poverty rate, since they focus on annual changes. The poverty rate begins to increase four years before divorce, peaking in the year of divorce. This pattern may reflect the effects of separation on the poverty rate prior to the actual divorce. It might also indicate that husband-wife families that become poor are more likely to experience marital disruption than those whose family income remains above the poverty level. After divorce, poverty rates begin to decrease. By six years after divorce, the poverty rate of divorced women is about the same as it was six years before divorce.

Finally, Table 3-7 presents data on how public assistance status changes over the ten-year period. Only a small proportion of married women are in

TABLE 3–7: *Public Assistance Status by Marital History, 1966 and 1976 (Weighted Percentages)*

Marital History	1966	Year (Number)	1976	(Number)
Married throughout	1%	(2,273)	2%	(2,259)
Recently divorced	6%	(172)	12%	(171)
Long-term divorced	21%	(170)	27%	(170)
Never married	12%	(164)	15%	(163)
Recently separated	9%	(101)	36%	(101)
Long-term separated	38%	(84)	49%	(84)
Remarried throughout	3%	(267)	3%	(266)
Remarried, divorced after 1967	2%	(81)	12%	(81)
Remarried, divorced in 1967	20%	(76)	8%	(76)
Other	7%	(572)	10%	(566)
Total, all cases	4%	(3,960)	6%	(3,937)

FIGURE 3-6: *Divorced Women's Poverty Rate Time Series Data*

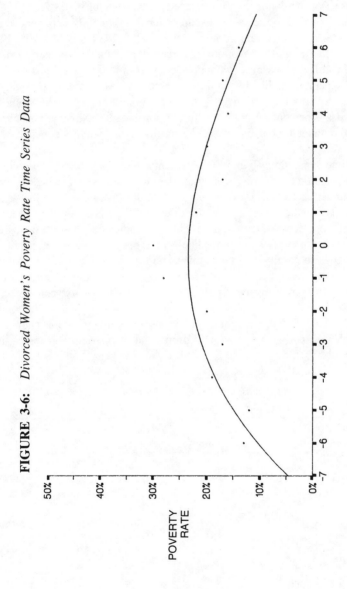

families receiving public assistance payments.[26] Married women who were about to separate or divorce were more likely than other married women to receive public assistance. Their rates of receiving public assistance increased even further after divorce or separation. High proportions of women who were unmarried at both time points (i.e., long-term divorced women, long-term separated women, and never-married women) received public assistance, and the proportions increased between 1966 and 1976. The evidence on the effects of remarriage is contradictory. Women who were divorced in 1967 and remarried in 1977 experienced a decline in their rate of receiving public assistance from 20% to 8%. However, women who divorced and remarried during the survey period were *more* likely to receive public assistance in 1976 (12%) than in 1966 (2%). Since remarriage would be expected to reduce reliance on public assistance, the latter finding is anomalous.

Time series data (Figure 3-7) do not provide a clear picture of the effects of divorce on public assistance status, since the proportion of women on public assistance fluctuates considerably, particularly after divorce. In general, it appears that women are more likely to receive public assistance after divorce than before. However, in four of the six years after divorce, the proportion of women receiving public assistance is relatively low (about 10%).

3.4 SUMMARY

The findings in this chapter confirm that divorce and remarriage are associated with changes in women's labor supply, earning power, and economic well-being. Specifically, the effects of divorce include increases in labor force participation rates and in annual hours, higher wages and earnings over the long term, lower family income, higher poverty rates and a greater likelihood of receiving public assistance. Remarriage is associated with lower labor force participation rates, fewer hours worked, lower annual earnings, higher family income, lower poverty rates, and less reliance on public assistance, relative to divorced women. The average divorced woman becomes more attached to the labor market as a result of increased economic need, while remarriage reduces both attachment to the labor market and economic need.

These results support the human capital argument described in Chapter 1, that women make trade-offs between work and spouse's income. The data presented in this chapter are only descriptive; no attempt has been made to explain these patterns. Whether these trade-offs are the result of rational choices (as human capital theory argues) or of structural or normative constraints, they have significant costs when marital disruption occurs. Most

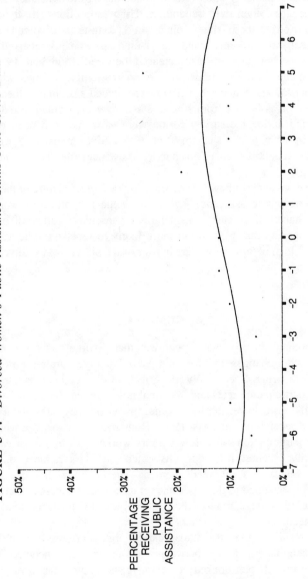

FIGURE 3-7: *Divorced Women's Public Assistance Status Time Series Data*

women experience a severe drop in their standard of living after marital disruption. Some improve their situation through remarriage, others through increased work activity. Some women apparently do not recover to any significant degree, even over the course of a decade. The high divorce rate and the costs of reliance on spouse's income for those who divorce suggest that married women can guarantee their economic security only by maintaining a strong attachment to the labor market. Data on younger cohorts of women suggest that young married women are more likely to work and to have careers than were previous cohorts of married women. The economic effects of divorce for cohorts of younger women may therefore not be as disastrous as they were for the cohort considered here.

The effects of separation include slightly higher labor force participation rates, lower wages and earnings over the long term, lower family income, higher poverty rates, and greater reliance on public assistance. Separated women are unlike divorced women in several ways: they are less likely to work; when they do work, they work fewer hours, receiving lower wages and earnings. Separated women also have a lower standard of living than divorced women. For some women, especially poor women, separation may be a permanent state. For other women, separation is a temporary transition phase between marriage and divorce. Economic difficulties are most acute immediately after separation. Weiss claims that "it is separation, not divorce, that disrupts the structure of the individual's social and emotional life."[27] For these women, some economic improvement may have occurred by the time of a divorce.

The use of the marital history measure has provided evidence on "causes" or "enabling conditions" of changes in marital status. Both working and receiving public assistance are associated with higher rates of marital dissolution. Married women who were about to separate or divorce were more likely to work or to receive public assistance while married than women who were to remain married. Perhaps working or receiving public assistance causes tensions which promote marital instability. There may also be "independence effects," i.e., women who have marital problems (not caused by work or public assistance) and who work or receive public assistance are more able to divorce or separate. It is also possible that women who anticipate marital disruption work before separating to prepare for the loss of spouse's earnings. The availability of longitudinal data has provided evidence on the nature of the relationship between marital history and economic variables. Marital history both depends on and affects economic outcomes.[28]

The life-course measure of marital history and the time series data identify long-term consequences of divorce, which cross-sectional and short-term longitudinal studies were unable to establish. Data on the long-term consequences of divorce suggest that many women partially recover from the economic hardship. While other studies found increases in labor force participation, hours worked, and earnings as a result of divorce, this study also finds an increase in wages. Divorced women who work improve their position in the labor market over the long term. For these women, this improvement partially counteracts the loss of spouse's income and raises their standard of living. How this improvement is achieved is the subject of the next few chapters.

One last, but important, finding should be mentioned. Divorced and never-married women tend to fare better than married women in the labor market (in terms of wages and earnings). However, they fare worse than married women on measures of economic well-being (family income, poverty status, and public assistance status). This disparity can be understood in two ways. The first and more obvious explanation is that the contribution of a spouse's earnings to the family income of married women is substantially greater than is the contribution of a divorced woman's own earnings to her family income. Divorced and never-married women have lower family income, because their earnings are still relatively low, compared to those of men. The second explanation is that among divorced and never-married women, there is a sharp distinction between those who work and those who do not.[29] A substantial proportion of those who work may support themselves adequately, although their standard of living is not as high as that of married women. Those who do not work (and perhaps some of those who do) may have to rely on public assistance, or on poverty-level earnings, and thus have a lower mean standard of living. This polarization is discussed again in Chapter 6. However, it is important to remember that analyses of working divorced women (such as those presented in the next two chapters) pertain to a relatively advantaged group of divorced women.

CHAPTER 4

Labor Supply

4.1 INTRODUCTION: ECONOMIC MODELS OF LABOR SUPPLY

Divorce increases women's total labor supply, as Chapter 3 indicates. Divorced women are more likely to work, and to work longer hours, than married women, because of economic need. This chapter develops models to account for marital history differences in women's labor supply. These models draw on economists' approaches to the study of labor force participation and hours worked. In the model for annual hours, labor market segmentation variables are also considered.

In the simple static model of labor supply, hours worked (H) depend on an individual's tastes for leisure (L) and for consumption goods (C) subject to several constraints. The individual's property (i.e., nonwork) income (V), as well as the prices of consumption goods (P) and of leisure hours (W, the hourly wage), determine the individual's budget constraint:

$$PC = WH + V$$

In other words, spending on consumer goods (PC) must equal the sum of work income (WH) and other income (V). An individual's tastes for leisure and consumption goods are represented by an indifference curve, which "shows different combinations of C and L that give the individual the same level of satisfaction."[1] Individuals are assumed to maximize utility (i.e., to achieve the optimal combination of C and L) subject to their budget constraint. Changes in budget constraints cause changes in consumption and leisure.

There are two types of changes—an income effect and a substitution effect. If a worker receives a wage increase, she can work fewer hours over the course of the year and receive the same total annual income. This *income effect* is the tendency of an individual to consume more leisure (i.e., to work less). However, an hour of leisure is also more costly after a wage increase; therefore there is also a negative *substitution effect* on leisure time. Since each hour of leisure time is consumed at the cost of a greater per-hour loss of wages, the individual may choose to work more and so consume less leisure. The net result of these opposing effects depends on the individual's taste for leisure (represented by her indifference curves). Individuals who value leisure more will work less; individuals who value work (and consumption) more will work more hours. Note also that if her relative wage drops low enough, an individual may find that *not* working maximizes utility. The point at which an individual is indifferent between working and not working is her reservation wage.

Marital history differences in labor supply are considered here in the context of a family labor supply model. Hours worked are assumed to depend on an individual's wage (*W*) and on earnings of other household members, as well as on (an unmeasured) taste for work (*E*). Earnings of other household members are treated as nonwork income (*V*) in the regression model:

$$H = a + bW + cV + E$$

This model ignores regional variation in prices (*P*) which affects the relative values of *W* and *V*. The model also ignores the effects of taxes, transfer income, cross-substitution effects, and time and money costs of transportation to work. While these factors are important in the development of sophisticated models of labor supply, the primary concern here is to account for marital history differences. This simple model will suffice for that purpose.

Before presenting results, several issues regarding estimation of the labor supply models need to be addressed. The first issue concerns the introduction of variables from the family labor supply model described above. The effects of marital history on labor supply will be estimated after controlling for the effects of hourly wage (W). However, the effects of earnings of other household members (V) will not be controlled for initially. Such earnings will be treated as part of the explanatory model to be introduced later. The second estimation problem concerns the measurement of the wage variable to be used in the model predicting annual hours worked.[2] Since the dependent variable, annual hours worked, refers to the year 1976, one could calculate a woman's wage in 1976 as total earnings divided by total hours. However, such a measure generally overestimates the effects of wage on hours. Because there is error in the measurement of annual hours worked, the correlation between wage and hours worked is artificially increased due to the positive correlation between errors in the two measures.

For that reason, wage at 1977 job is used, since it is an independent measure of wage (not derived as earnings/hours).[3]

As described in Chapter 3, there is a selection bias involved in analyzing hours, earnings, and wage data only for those who work. The effects of some explanatory variables would appear to be stronger than they actually are, because some of the independent variables may affect both the likelihood of working and the dependent variable (hours, earnings, or wages). For example, education may affect both the probability of working and the number of hours worked among working women. In all analyses restricted to working women, a statistical technique is employed to correct for this kind of selection bias.[4] First, a logistic regression model is developed to predict a woman's probability of working, similar to the analysis of labor force status described below. (See Appendix D for the specific models used to estimate the correction for selection bias in the hours, earnings, and wage equations.) The predicted probability of working is then included as a control variable in each of the explanatory models developed for annual hours, annual earnings, and hourly wage.

It should be noted that this approach will provide a conservative test of the structural model. It may not be appropriate to control for selectivity in a structural model, which measures the effects of demand for labor.[5] Since demand reflects factors which pull individuals into the labor market, structural models are not concerned with individualistic factors predisposing people to work. Differential demand for particular types of employees may provide incentives for particular groups of people to work or not to work. If so, what appears to be selection bias (a predisposition for a particular type of person to work) may also be interpreted as a result of demand factors (a preference by employers for a particular type of employee).

There is a second type of selection bias that might affect the analyses. Marital history and the dependent variables may be affected by other background characteristics predisposing women to marry, divorce, or remarry. For example, divorced women who have little work experience may have low wages, and as a result, may be more likely to remarry than other divorced women. Consequently, wages of divorced women may appear to be high, when in fact some divorced women who earn low wages have remarried. To account for potential selection bias by marital history, models were also developed to predict the probability of marriage for all women, of divorce for women who ever married, and of remarriage for women who ever divorced. The predicted probabilities of marriage, of divorce, and of remarriage were then used as corrections for these types of selection bias. In all the models developed in this study, including the correction for these types of selection bias had no meaningful effect on results after including the correction for nonworking women in the equations. This finding is not surprising, since the factors affecting the probability of working and those affecting marital history may be strongly related. (See Appendix D.)

In the model of labor force participation, women who worked any hours in 1976 are considered to be in the labor force; women who did not work in 1976 are considered out of the labor force. Because of the limited dispersion of this dichotomous dependent variable, multiple regression techniques are inappropriate. Logistic regression corrects for this problem, and is employed here.[6]

4.2   EFFECTS OF MARITAL HISTORY ON LABOR FORCE PARTICIPATION

In Chapter 3, differences among marital history groups were described without controlling for race. In the explanatory model developed here, the effects of marital history are tested controlling for the effects of race. A *description* of the effects of marital history must include the effects of race, since marital history depends, to an important degree, on race. An *explanation* of the effects of marital history ought to control for the effects of race, since race is not an explanation, except at the most superficial level, for differences among marital history categories. The justification for controlling for race in the explanatory models is both theoretical and empirical. From a theoretical standpoint, this analysis is concerned with accounting for differences among marital history groups. Such differences should be evaluated controlling for the effects of differences in racial composition among the marital history categories. From an empirical standpoint, controlling for race is important, since the NLS sample is stratified by race, with blacks overrepresented. The inclusion of race as a control variable will prevent any bias that the sampling design might otherwise introduce into the estimates.[7]

In the marital history model, continuously married women represent the reference category, and four dummy variables represent the other marital history categories.[8] The effects of race are represented by the variable "nonwhite" (coded 1 for blacks and "others" and 0 for whites).[9]

As expected, divorced and never-married women have higher labor force participation rates than married women (see Table 4-1, column [1]). These effects may reflect the greater economic need of these single women and/or their greater taste for work, but this model does not provide a direct assessment of the relative importance of these two factors.

TABLE 4–1:
Explanatory Models of Labor Force Participation

	Dependent Variable		
	Labor Force Participation, 1976 (N = 3,611) Logistic Regression Coefficients (standard error in parentheses)		
Independent Variables	Marital History Variables	Human Capital Variables	Individualist Model
	[1]	[2]	[3]
Nonwhite	− .01	.18*	.32***
	(.08)	(.08)	(.09)
Marital History Variables			
Recently divorced[a]	.92***	.92***	.93***
	(.18)	(.19)	(.20)
Long-term divorced[a]	.79***	.82***	.79***
	(.18)	(.19)	(.20)
Never married	.78***	.72***	.71***
	(.20)	(.20)	(.21)
Other marital history[b]	.09	.23**	.25**
	(.08)	(.08)	(.09)
Human Capital Variables			
Education		.11***	.05***
		(.02)	(.02)
Education, squared		—	—
Years since school		.10*	.03
		(.06)	(.06)
Years since school, squared		− .002*	− .001
		(.001)	(.001)
Family Role Variables			
Any hours worked by other household members			—
Number of hours worked by other household members			—

[a] Differences between the coefficients for the long-term divorced and the recently divorced are not statistically significant in any of the three equations presented here.

[b] Two-tailed significance test.

[c] The effect of this variable is not statistically significant using a one-tailed test, since its effect is not in the predicted direction. The effect of this variable *is* staistically significant if a two-tailed test is used.

(Continued on next page)

TABLE 4–1—*Continued*

Independent Variables	Dependent Variable		
	Labor Force Participation, 1976 (N = 3,611) Logistic Regression Coefficients (standard error in parentheses)		
	Marital History Variables	Human Capital Variables	Individualist Model
	[1]	[2]	[3]
Earnings of other household members (Ln)			.02^c (.01)
Egalitarian gender attitudes			.14*** (.01)
Any children			—
Number of children			−.19*** (.03)
Total fertility			—
Age			—
Age, squared			—
Chi-square	58.31***	181.88***	405.41***
degrees of fredom	(6)	(9)	(12)
Change in chi-square	NA	123.57***	223.53***

Ln = Natural logarithm transformation
— = Variable considered for entry into equation, but did not meet significance level criterion (p < .05).
  * p < .05
 ** p < .01
*** p < .001

4.3 EXPLANATORY MODELS OF LABOR FORCE PARTICIPATION

This section considers whether human capital and/or family role variables account for marital history differences in women's labor force participation. (Structural models generally do not analyze labor force status, since labor market segmentation measures are not available for nonworkers.) Models which account for labor force participation have generally used human capital and family role variables, since tastes for work and leisure are assumed to be reflected in an individual's level of investment in human capital.[10] Individuals who have greater investments in human capital may be more committed to working, and are more likely to be able to obtain high-paying jobs. Human capital variables in the model presented here represent the individual's taste for work; family role variables represent economic constraints or incentives, and may also reflect tastes for work.

Results are discussed separately for sets of variables, to provide an appropriate theoretical context. The effects of individual variables within sets are discussed where it is relevant. Variables that were considered for inclusion in the equation, but that did not have statistically significant effects and were dropped, are listed without coefficients. In several instances, variables which did not have statistically significant effects were retained for theoretical reasons (see tables in this chapter and Chapter 5).

In the human capital model (Table 4-1, column [2]), women who have more years of education, as expected, are more likely to be in the labor force. A curvilinear relationship was tested but was not significant. As a measure of potential work experience, "years since school" has a positive effect on the likelihood of labor force participation. However, this effect weakens over time, as indicated by the negative coefficient of the squared term. Adding the human capital variables to the model does not account for the higher labor force participation rates of either category of divorced women relative to continuously married women, while the difference between never-married women and continuously married women decreases slightly (compare Table 4-1, columns [1] and [2]). This finding indicates that the higher labor force participation rates of single women do not reflect their greater taste for work as reflected by investments in human capital.[11]

Next, aspects of family labor supply are considered (Table 4-1, column [3]). This individualist model is discussed here in some detail, since a variety of measures were tested and since some of the findings are anomalous. Whether anyone in the household worked and the number of hours worked by others have no effect on a woman's labor force status. These variables were expected to have a negative effect, particularly for married women. However, tests for interactions between these variables and the marital history variables did not reveal any significant differences in the effects of these variables by marital history (data not shown). Earnings of other household members have an unexpected positive effect on the likelihood of working. Women in households where earnings of others are relatively high are *more* likely to work than women in households where other earnings are relatively low.[12] Most previous research predicts a *negative* effect of other earnings,[13] since earnings of others are expected to raise a woman's reservation wage, making her less likely to work.

Several reformulations of the model were considered to clear up this discrepancy (data not shown). Interactions between earnings of other household members and marital history were tested to see if the effects of other earnings varied by marital history. None of these interactions was significant, suggesting that all women, regardless of marital history, are more likely to work when others in the household have relatively high earnings. Human capital variables were removed from the model to test whether a negative effect of other earnings might be suppressed as a result of controlling for human capital variables. However, other earnings have a positive effect even before human capital variables are entered. A measure of per capita earnings of others (i.e., other earnings divided by the size of the household) was also considered, to account for differences in economic need among households. This variable had an effect in the expected negative direction, although the effect was not statistically significant. The latter finding suggests that households in which earnings of others are relatively high are larger households, and that in larger households there is more incentive for a woman to work (i.e., economic need is greater).

Two other family role variables have a significant effect on labor force participation. Women who have egalitarian gender attitudes are much more likely to work, and women who have larger numbers of children are less likely to work. (Presence of children also has a negative effect on labor force participation, but this effect becomes insignificant when number of children is included in the equation.) Total fertility[14] and age have no significant effects after controlling for variables already in the model.

The addition of family role variables to the human capital model has no appreciable impact on the marital history effects (compare Table 4-1, columns [2] and [3]). Differences in family situations do not account for the difference between single women and married women in their likelihood of being in the labor force. Perhaps better measures of family roles would explain this difference, but as can be best determined from these data, "singleness" by itself is a strong predictor of labor force participation.

The remaining effects of marital history on the likelihood of labor force participation may be due to differences in the responsiveness of women in different marital history categories to human capital or family role factors. For example, highly educated divorced women may be more likely to work than highly educated married women. To address this possibility, interaction terms were created to allow the effect of each variable in the model to vary by marital history (data not shown). Rather than examine each interaction term for statistical significance, a "protected" significance test was conducted. It was first determined whether a set of interactions (between one marital history variable and all the other variables in the model) added significantly to chi-square for the equation. Only if a set of interactions was significant were individual interaction terms examined and interpreted.

Four sets of interactions (one each for the recently divorced, long-term divorced, never married, and other marital history) were tested (data not shown). The findings indicate that the model of labor force participation is the same for married women and recently divorced women. The positive effect of egalitarian gender attitudes on labor force participation is weaker for long-term divorced women and never-married women than for married women.

This finding suggests that regardless of their gender attitudes, long-term divorced women and never-married women are forced into the labor market by economic necessity. The negative effect of number of children is stronger for never-married women than for other women. Never-married women who have children may have more difficulty finding child care than married women.[15] In addition, children may prevent accumulation of human capital sufficient to support the families of never-married women, especially since unwed mothers tend to have children at a young age. Divorced women who have children may have more options for child care and therefore may be able to accumulate human capital more easily.[16]

The possibility that the effects of variables in the model differ by race was also considered. Among nonwhites, long-term divorced, never-married, and "other" women are less likely to work than continuously married women (data not shown). Controlling for these interactions has the effect of increasing the coefficients for these three marital history groups, since among whites, women in these three groups are *more* likely to work than continuously married women. This racial difference in the effects of marital history may reflect the effects of racial discrimination and/or a greater reliance on public assistance among single nonwhite women (see discussion in Chapter 6). Interactions of other variables with race were not significant.

In summary, the human capital/family role model accounts for some variation in labor force participation, but does not account for the effects of marital history on labor force participation. The marital history variables therefore reflect the effects of differences in economic need and in taste for work between married women and divorced or never-married women.

4.4 EFFECTS OF MARITAL HISTORY ON ANNUAL HOURS

The second aspect of women's labor supply that will be considered in this chapter is hours worked. There are two views on the determinants of time inputs to work. According to the human capital approach, workers adjust their hours of work according to individual characteristics (e.g., their taste for leisure, other demands on their time, their economic need), subject to a wage constraint. Another view is that time inputs to work are determined by institutional factors. The prevalence of seasonal and part-time work varies among industries, firms, and jobs. This structural approach does not rule out supply-side effects. Both supply and demand affect an individual's time inputs to work.[17]

Hours worked are expected to differ by marital history because it is assumed that single women have greater economic need than married women. However, it is also possible that employers prefer to hire single women rather than married women for year-round, full-time work or for jobs that often require overtime work. Both views will be explored here.

First, a marital history model is tested, then explanatory models are considered to account for marital history differences. The model developed here explicitly controls for the effects of hourly wage on hours worked. Dummy variables for the marital history categories are used to predict annual hours in 1976, after controlling for the effects of wage and race. In this context, labor market segmentation variables reflect demand for labor, human capital variables reflect tastes for work (controlling for their effect on wages), and family role variables reflect both tastes for work and budget constraints.

Women work more hours at higher wages, but at a declining rate (note the positive coefficient for the effect of wage, and the negative coefficient for the effect of wage, squared) (Table 4-2, column [1]). However, the variation accounted for by such effects is fairly small, indicating that demand factors or other supply factors play an important role. Although the effect of race is not statistically significant, the variable "nonwhite" is retained in the model as a control variable, for reasons described above (see discussion in Section 4.2). In column [2], the effects of marital history variables are tested. Since the dependent variable is the natural logarithm of annual hours, and since the coefficients are relatively low (below .25), these unstandardized coefficients may be interpreted (approximately) as percentage changes in annual hours associated with a unit change in the independent variable. As expected, never-married women and both categories of divorced women work significantly more hours than continuously married women—about 24% more for never-married women, and about 18% more for divorced women.

The relationship between marital history and hours worked among working women may reflect the effects of marital history on both the probability of working and on hours worked. This selection bias would artificially inflate the estimates of the effects of marital history.[18] A correction for this kind of selection bias was introduced (see column [3] of Table 4-2 and discussion in Appendix D). The correction for selection bias slightly reduces the coefficients of recently divorced and never-married women, indicating that a small part of the effects observed without this correction (Table 4-2, column [2]) is due to the effects of marital history on labor force participation rather than on hours worked. However, the marital history variables have a significant positive effect on hours worked, even after controlling for marital history differences in the likelihood of labor force participation. Single women (i.e., divorced and never-married women) are more likely to work, and to work longer hours than married women.

TABLE 4–2: *Explanatory Models of Annual Hours*

	Dependent Variable						
	Natural Logarithm of Annual Hours Worked, 1976 (N = 1,563) Metric Regression Coefficients (standard error in parentheses)						
Independent Variables	Wage	Marital History Variables	Correction for selection bias	Labor Market Segmentation Variables	Human Capital Variables	Structural Model	Individualist Model
	[1]	[2]	[3]	[4]	[5]	[6]	[7]
Wage (Ln), 1977	.54***	.56***	.52***	.27**	.13	.15*	.38***
	(.09)	(.09)	(.09)	(.09)	(.09)	(.09)	(.09)
Wage (Ln), 1977, squared	−.09**	−.11**	−.11***	−.08**	−.08**	−.08**	−.12***
	(.03)	(.03)	(.03)	(.03)	(.03)	(.03)	(.03)
Nonwhite	.04	.03	.01	.01	.03	.08**	.09**
	(.03)	(.03)	(.03)	(.03)	(.03)	(.04)	(.04)
Marital History Variables							
Recently divorced[a]		.17**	.15**	.14**	.14**	.13*	.14**
		(.06)	(.06)	(.06)	(.06)	(.06)	(.06)
Long-term divorced[a]		.18**	.18**	.16**	.13*	.14**	.16**
		(.06)	(.06)	(.06)	(.06)	(.06)	(.06)
Never married		.24***	.22***	.20***	.14*	.16**	.19**
		(.07)	(.07)	(.06)	(.06)	(.07)	(.07)
Other marital history[b]		.03	.04	.03	.004	.00	.01
		(.03)	(.03)	(.03)	(.03)	(.03)	(.04)
Correction for selection bias			.59***	.57***	.34***	−.37	−.44
			(.12)	(.12)	(.12)	(.22)	(.23)
Labor Market Segmentation Variables							
Job characteristics:							
(a) Decision latitude				—	—	—	
(b) Union membership[c]				.07*	.08*	.08*	
				(.04)	(.04)	(.04)	
(c) Job Insecurity				—	—	—	
(d) Supervisory status				—	—	—	
Firm size (Ln)[c]				.07***	.06***	.06***	
				(.01)	(.01)	(.01)	
Core Industry				.11***	.12***	.11***	
				(.03)	(.03)	(.03)	

[a] Differences between the coefficients for the long-term divorced and the recently divorced are not statistically significant in any of the six equations presented here.

[b] Two-tailed significance test.

[c] Mean substitution used. See discussion in Chapter 2.

(Continued on next page)

TABLE 4–2 — *Continued*

			Dependent Variable				
			Natural Logarithm of Annual Hours Worked, 1976 (N = 1,563) Metric Regression Coefficients (standard error in parentheses)				
Independent Variables	Wage	Marital History Variables	Correction for selection bias	Labor Market Segmentation Variables	Human Capital Variables	Structural Model	Individualist Model
	[1]	[2]	[3]	[4]	[5]	[6]	[7]
Human Capital Variables							
Education					—	—	—
Education, squared					—	—	—
Years of work experience					.05*** (.01)	.05*** (.01)	.05*** (.01)
Years of work experience, squared					−.001*** (.0002)	−.001*** (.0002)	−.001*** (.0002)
Received occupational training					—	—	—
Occupational status					.006*** (.001)	.007*** (.001)	.007*** (.001)
Family Role Variables							
Any other earners in household						—	—
Earnings of other household members (Ln)						−.004 (.004)	−.004 (.004)
Egalitarian gender attitudes						.03*** (.01)	.04*** (.01)
Any children						—	—
Number of children						—	—
Total fertility						—	—
Age						—	—
Age, squared						—	—
R^2	.06***	.07***	.09***	.14***	.19***	.20***	.15***
Change in R^2	NA	.01***	.02***	.05***	.05***	.01***	−.05***

Ln = Natural logarithm transformation.
— = Variable considered for entry into equation, but did not meet significance level criterion ($p < .05$).
* $p < .05$
** $p < .01$
*** $p < .001$

4.5 EXPLANATORY MODELS OF ANNUAL HOURS

The explanatory model developed here and also employed in Chapter 5 is based on a structural view of the labor market. Both individual characteristics and labor market segmentation variables play a role in determining labor market outcomes and in accounting for differences among marital history categories. While these variables have been subjected to extensive empirical tests of their ability to account for labor market outcomes, there is disagreement about how to integrate them into a single structural model. Some individual characteristics may be determined by structural constraints, while structural location may be affected by individual characteristics. As a result, the interpretation of the effects of a particular variable may depend on the theoretical perspective taken. For example, supervisory status may reflect a worker's abilities, interests, and experience (i.e., the human capital interpretation), or it may reflect tenure in a large firm that has a job ladder (i.e., the internal labor market interpretation). While supervisory status may reflect both supply and demand factors, sorting out the relative effects of each is difficult, since supply factors interact with demand factors (i.e., the effect of one depends on the other).[19] A dynamic model that considers such interactions may offer a more realistic view of the labor market than that provided by the structural model considered here. However, the development of an integrated, dynamic model is beyond the scope of this study.

The approach taken here is guided by a provisional hypothesis. Different labor market segments define different ranges of possible outcomes; within these ranges, individual characteristics (human capital, family role) may make a difference.[20] To test this model, sets of variables are added to the marital history equation hierarchically. Labor market segmentation variables are introduced into the equation, followed by human capital and family role variables. This approach assumes that individual attributes account for labor market outcomes within constraints determined by structural features of the labor market. The full structural model includes all three sets of variables (labor market segmentation, human capital, and family role variables), while the full individualist model includes only the human capital and family role variables.

Differences in hours worked may reflect differences in demand for labor between primary and secondary jobs. Primary jobs are more likely to be year-round, full-time jobs and are more likely to require overtime work. Secondary jobs are more likely to involve seasonal work, frequent layoffs, and part-time work. If divorced and never-married women are more likely to be in primary jobs than married women, this difference may account for their higher mean hours worked. While labor market segmentation variables (Table 4-2, column [4]) reduce differences in hours worked, this reduction is modest. An analysis of the effects of individual variables (data not shown) indicates that this small reduction is due primarily to differences in firm size. Never-married and divorced women are more likely to work in large firms (which require longer hours of work) than married women. The labor market segmentation variables perform poorly in accounting for annual hours, explaining only 5% of the variance, after controlling for marital history, wage, race, and the correction for selection bias.[21]

According to a structural approach, wages and hours are codetermined characteristics of jobs, set by employers; hence, using wages to predict hours, as was done here, is technically inappropriate. To the extent that this argument is correct, however, one would hypothesize that introducing measures of labor market segmentation ought to account for the relationship between wages and hours worked. This hypothesis was only partially supported (see Table 4-2; note the reduction in the coefficient for 1977 wage from column [3] to column [4]).

The assumptions of human capital theory suggest that variation in investments in human capital should explain variation in hours worked. Hours worked are assumed to reflect individual choice, subject to a wage constraint, as explained earlier. Not only are tastes for work reflected by an individual's level of investment in human capital, but greater investments in human capital increase a worker's value to her employer, which should be reflected in annual hours. Valued workers are more likely to be required to work full-time and to work year-round, since there are fixed administrative costs for each employee. Also, experienced employees are more productive at the margin than inexperienced ones. These factors encourage employers to require longer hours of work from valued employees rather than to hire new employees on a part-time basis. Although it is not a human capital measure, occupational status is also considered in this model, since it is an important explanatory variable in earlier sociological research on the relationship between marital status and women's work patterns.[22] Women who have more years of education, women who have more years of work experience, women who have enrolled in occupational training programs, and women who have higher occupational status are expected to work more hours than other women.

The model incorporating human capital variables indicates that work experience and occupational status are positively associated with hours worked (see Table 4-2, column [5]). Women who have more years of work experience work more hours, though at a declining rate (even after controlling for the indirect effect of experience on hours through wages). Neither occupational training nor years of education has a statistically significant effect on hours worked, controlling for wage. However, introducing human capital variables reduces from 20% to 14% the difference in hours worked between continuously married and never-married women, and slightly reduces the difference between long-term divorced and married women. These reductions are primarily due to differences in work experience (data not shown). The addition of human capital variables has no effect on the coefficient for recently divorced women.

Since the effects of family roles are only indirectly reflected in human capital variables, the direct effects of family role variables are explicitly considered in the full individualist model. Hours worked may be subject to conditions such as hours worked by others in the household, number and ages of children, and gender attitudes. Surprisingly, among these variables, only gender attitudes have a statistically significant effect on hours worked. Egalitarian gender attitudes are associated with more hours worked, but do not account for any of the marital history differences (Table 4-2, column [6]). Earnings of other household members is retained in the equation because of its theoretical importance for the labor supply model. Although its effect is not statistically significant, it has the expected negative effect on hours worked (see discussion in Chapter 1). Considering this finding in conjunction with those from the model of labor force participation (Table 4-1), it appears that women in households where earnings of others are high are more likely to work than other women, but work fewer hours than other working women. This pattern of results illustrates the complex relationship between economic need and labor supply. Apparently, households where other earnings are relatively high have greater economic need, which encourages women to work. However, these incentives are not strong enough to induce women to work long hours.

Since it might be hypothesized that the effects of other family role variables depend on whether or not a woman is married, tests for interactions between these variables and the marital history variables were performed (data not shown). None was significant. Nor did the effects of variables in the full model (Table 4-2, column [6]) differ by marital history.[23] Furthermore, neither the effects of marital history nor the effects of other variables in the model differ by race (data not shown).[24]

The full model (Table 4-2, column [6]) accounts for only 20% of the variation in hours worked. Several factors may account for the low explanatory power of this model. First, some measures used here may not be sensitive enough. Second, the model may be poorly specified. Variables left out of the model may account for a significant portion of the remaining unexplained variation in hours worked. Finally, variation in hours worked may be idiosyncratic, subject to individual variation in tastes for hours of work. The latter explanation, unsatisfying as it is sociologically, may be the most important. Other studies of hours worked also explain only a small proportion of variation.[25]

Finally, an individualist model was examined (Table 4-2, column [7]), in which human capital and family role variables are included without labor market segmentation variables. A comparison of this model with the full structural model (Table 4-2, column [6]) indicates that the exclusion of segmentation variables significantly reduces the explanatory power of the equation for hours worked (lowering explained variance from 20% to 15%). However, the individualist model is almost as effective as the structural model in accounting for marital history differences. (Note that the coefficients in Table 4-2, column [7] are only slightly higher than those in column [6].)

4.6 SUMMARY OF FINDINGS ON LABOR SUPPLY

The models of labor supply considered here confirm the hypothesis that divorce increases the labor supply of women. Surprisingly, the magnitude of this effect is about the same for the long-term divorced and for the recently divorced. Apparently, the effect of divorce on labor supply occurs quickly and reaches its maximum within a few short years of the divorce (this conclusion is also supported by the analyses in Chapter 3). In response to economic need, these adjustments in labor supply can be achieved within a few years by a large proportion of divorced women. For this reason, even cross-sectional studies comparing currently married to currently divorced women have found that divorce is associated with increased labor supply.

To go beyond confirming this finding, the analyses in this chapter attempted to account for the effects of marital history on labor supply. The most complete model considered could not explain any significant portion of the differences in labor supply by marital history. Among the labor market segmentation variables, firm size has small effects on marital history differences, suggesting that large firms have a slight preference for divorced and never-married women in year-round full-time work. Among the human capital variables, work experience partially accounts for the difference in hours worked between married and never-married women. Work experience may be a measure of never-married women's greater taste for work, or greater work experience may enable never-married women to be hired in more secure full-time, year-round work. While differences in family roles were expected to be important determinants of marital history differences in labor supply, the indicators included here were relatively ineffective. The weakness of the family role variables might be due to the use of indicators which were poorly measured, or to the use of the wrong indicators. Until better measures are found, or new indicators employed, the analyses presented here leave one to conclude that the marital history differences reflect some combination of economic need and taste for work, the relative importance of which cannot be determined. Given the findings in Chapter 3, some divorced women clearly had a greater taste for work even while married (given their higher labor force participation rate while married). Nevertheless, it seems clear that divorce also results in further increases in labor supply in response to economic need.

CHAPTER 5

Personal Income

In this chapter, structural, human capital, and family role variables are used to account for the earnings and wage advantages of divorced and never-married women. To the extent that adequate measures of these factors are included in the analyses, the marital history effects should be accounted for by the combination of variables employed here. The ability of the labor market segmentation variables to account for the effects of marital history is expected to be weak, while an individualist model (i.e., human capital and family role variables) is expected to account for a significant portion of these effects. This prediction is based on the assumption that the effects of marital history on income are due to (supply-side) differences in labor force behavior and not to (demand-side) differences in employer behavior.

Models of both annual earnings and hourly wage are developed in this chapter. While both are measures of economic rewards, annual earnings include the effects of individual differences in hours worked over the course of a year. Hourly wage, on the other hand, is a measure of earning power and, according to human capital theory, represents the marginal productivity of workers. Since married women, on average, have less incentive to work long hours than divorced or never-married women, one would expect earnings differences among marital history categories to be stronger than wage differences.

5.1 EFFECTS OF MARITAL HISTORY ON ANNUAL EARNINGS

In the analysis of annual earnings, the effects of marital history variables are estimated after controlling for the effect of race (Table 5-1, column [1]). Never-married women, recently divorced women, and long-term divorced women have large earnings advantages over married women. By comparison, racial differences in earnings (roughly an 18% disadvantage for nonwhites) are considerably smaller.

As was noted in the analysis of annual hours worked, the effects of marital history may be due, at least in part, to selection bias. If factors

TABLE 5–1: *Explanatory Models of Annual Earnings*

	Dependent Variable					
	Natural Logarithm of Annual Earnings, 1976 (N = 1,703) Metric Regression Coefficients (standard error in parentheses)					
Independent Variables	Marital History Variables	Correction for selection bias	Labor Market Segmentation Variables	Human Capital Variables	Structural Model	Individualist Model
	[1]	[2]	[3]	[4]	[5]	[6]
Nonwhite	−.18***	−.22***	−.08	−.08	−.07	−.08
	(.06)	(.05)	(.05)	(.05)	(.05)	(.05)
Marital History Variables						
Recently divorced[a]	.46***	.38***	.34***	.31***	.38***	.41***
	(.11)	(.10)	(.10)	(.09)	(.09)	(.10)
Long-term divorced[a]	.53***	.46***	.36***	.24**	.30***	.38***
	(.11)	(.11)	(.10)	(.09)	(.10)	(.10)
Never married	.59***	.45***	.38***	.10	.18*	.22**
	(.12)	(.11)	(.10)	(.10)	(.11)	(.11)
Other marital history[b]	−.03	.02	.00	−.04	−.01	.02
	(.06)	(.06)	(.05)	(.05)	(.05)	(.06)
Correction for		2.56***	1.83***	1.14***	1.13***	1.30***
selection bias		(.18)	(.17)	(.19)	(.19)	(.20)
Labor Market Segmentation Variables Job characteristics:						
(a) Decision latitude			—	—	—	
(b) Union membership[c]			.32***	.22***	.22***	
			(.07)	(.06)	(.06)	
(c) Job insecurity			−.48***	−.004	.00	
			(.15)	(.15)	(.15)	
(d) Supervisory status			.67***	.18	.18	
			(.12)	(.12)	(.12)	
Firm size (Ln)[c]			.12***	.09***	.09***	
			(.01)	(.01)	(.01)	
Core industry			.39***	.33***	.33***	
			(.05)	(.05)	(.05)	

[a] Differences between the coefficients for the long-term divorced and the recently divorced are not statistically significant in any of the six equations presented here.

[b] Two-tailed significance test.

[c] Mean substitution used. See discussion in Chapter 2.

(Continued on next page)

TABLE 5–1–*Continued*

Independent Variables	Marital History Variables	Correction for selection bias	Labor Market Segmentation Variables	Human Capital Variables	Structural Model	Individualist Model
	[1]	[2]	[3]	[4]	[5]	[6]
Human Capital Variables						
Education				.001	.00	−.01
				(.01)	(.01)	(.01)
Education, squared				—	—	—
Years of work experience				.03***	.03***	.04***
				(.003)	(.003)	(.003)
Years of work experience, squared				—	—	—
Received occupational training				.08*	.08*	.11*
				(.05)	(.05)	(.05)
Occupational status				.02***	.02***	.02***
				(.002)	(.002)	(.002)
Family Role Variables						
Any other earners in household				—	—	—
Earnings of other household members (Ln)					.01*	.02**
					(.006)	(.006)
Egalitarian gender attitudes					—	—
Any children					—	—
Number of children					—	—
Total fertility					—	—
Age					—	—
Age, squared					—	—
R^2	.04***	.14***	.27***	.37***	.37***	.30***
Change in R^2	NA	.10***	.13***	.10***	.001*	−.07***

Ln = Natural logarithm transformation.

— = Variable considered for entry into equation, but did not meet significance level criterion ($p < .05$).

* $p < .05$

** $p < .01$

*** $p < .001$

predisposing women to work are correlated with both marital history and annual earnings, the effects of marital history on annual earnings are artificially inflated. Introducing the correction for selection bias (Table 5-1, column [2]) reduces the effects of the marital history variables. The earnings advantage for recently divorced women is reduced to 46%, for long-term divorced women to 58%, and for never-married women to 57%.[1] While the factors predisposing women to work partially account for the earnings advantages of divorced and never-married women, a significant earnings advantage over married women remains to be explained.

The larger earnings advantage for the long-term divorced relative to the recently divorced is consistent with the evidence presented in Chapter 3 that the effects of divorce on earnings increase over time. While the earnings difference between these two categories is not statistically significant, an analysis of divorced women predicting 1976 annual earnings from years since divorce indicates that earnings do increase over time, but at a declining rate (data not shown). Apparently women who divorce and who remain divorced over a long period are able to "recover" from the negative economic impact of marriage (and, in many cases, of child rearing) and return to a level of earnings comparable to that of women who never married.

5.2   EXPLANATORY MODELS OF ANNUAL EARNINGS

The earnings advantages of divorced and never-married women might be explained by their greater likelihood of working in advantaged labor market segments. To test this possibility, labor market segmentation variables are added to the explanatory model (Table 5-1, column [3]). The effects of marital history are partially explained by this set of variables, although all coefficients remain statistically significant. Most of this explanatory power derives from the inclusion of firm size in the equation. Divorced and never-married women are more likely to work in larger firms than married women. Never-married women also are more likely to work in jobs with more decision latitude than married women. These results for divorced and never-married women suggest that there are demand differences by marital history, a finding that was not expected. Employers in advantaged labor market segments may prefer divorced and never-married women over married women as employees. The argument that these patterns reflect differential demand cannot be definitive, however, since these patterns might also reflect self-selection. Divorced and never-married women may select or seek out more desirable jobs in large firms so as to maximize their earning power.

The human capital approach assumes that earnings variation among women can be accounted for by differences in their education and/or work histories. These, in turn, are seen as reflecting the different levels of investment in human capital by women who have different marital histories. Adding the human capital variables to the model reduces the earnings advantages of both categories of divorced women (Table 5-1, column [4]). There are no statistically significant earnings differences between married and never-married women, after controlling for labor market segmentation and human capital variables.

These reductions in the effects of marital history are primarily due to the greater work experience of never-married and divorced women. To provide further detail about the effect of work experience, an additional work history measure was tested (data not shown). Withdrawals from the labor force during the 10 years of the study period (data were not available for all women on previous labor force withdrawals) had a negative effect on annual earnings, and slightly reduced the earnings advantage for long-term divorced women. Long-term divorced women were less likely to withdraw from the labor force between 1967 and 1977, presumably for economic reasons.

The only family role variable that has a significant effect on women's earnings is earnings of other household members (Table 5-1, column [5]). The amount of earnings of others in the household is positively associated with a woman's earnings. When both spouses work, spouses' earnings are positively correlated (see discussion in Chapter 1). However, controlling for earnings of others does not explain or account for the earnings advantage of divorced women or of never-married women; rather, the advantage increases slightly. As explained in the discussion of findings on labor force participation, this variable raises a woman's asking wage. Divorced women have higher earnings than might be expected given that they are less likely than married women to have other highly paid earners in their household. In other words, the difference in earnings between married and divorced women (and between married and never-married women) would be expected to be larger than it is. This expectation is based on the assumption that divorced and never-married women are likely to have a lower asking wage than married women, and therefore are more likely to feel constrained to accept even a low-paying job. Divorced women have higher earnings than would be expected, given that they are subject to this constraint.

The remaining effects of marital history on earnings may be due to differential returns to labor market segmentation, human capital, or family role variables. Tests of interactions of explanatory variables with marital history (see description of procedure in Chapter 4) were not significant (data not shown). Interactions of race with all variables in the model, including marital history variables, were also tested. Two interactions were significant: nonwhites have lower returns to total experience than whites, and do not benefit from union membership as much as whites. These differences in returns, however, do not significantly reduce the remaining marital history differences with respect to earnings.

The full structural model (Table 5-1, column [5]) is more successful at accounting for the earnings advantage of some marital history groups than of others. The model accounts for 65% of the earnings advantage of never-married women, about 40% of the earnings advantage of the long-term divorced, and none of the earnings advantage of the recently divorced (compare column [5] with column [2]). These differences in the explanatory power of the model may reflect differences among marital history categories in the degree to which women's careers were planned. A high proportion of never-married women presumably expected to work, and have continuous work histories. Consequently, their earnings advantage over married women is accounted for by the standard measures of human capital and of demand for labor. The earnings advantage of divorced women, whose careers are more likely to reflect adjustments to an unexpected event, is not accounted for by the standard measures. Divorced women may make adjustments in their orientation to work not reflected in the individual characteristics measured here. Employers, believing that long-term divorced women are less likely to remarry, may favor such women in ways not reflected in the measures of demand considered here. Divorce seems to have effects on earnings not accounted for by the human capital, family role, or labor market segmentation variables considered here.

To provide a comparison of the effectiveness of the individualist and structural models, the earnings equation was re-estimated (Table 5-1, column [6]) without the labor market segmentation variables. This individualist model explains significantly less variance than the structural model (30% vs. 37%). Furthermore, the marital history effects are somewhat stronger in the individualist model than in the structural model, suggesting that including the labor market segmentation variables in the equation significantly improves the power of the model to explain marital history differences in earnings.

5.3   EFFECTS OF MARITAL HISTORY ON HOURLY WAGE

Since divorced women work more hours per year than married women, it is not surprising that their annual earnings are also higher. However, divorced women may also have higher hourly wages than married women, especially over the long-term, as predicted in Chapter 1. Models were constructed to predict hourly wage at current job in 1977 (Table 5-2). These analyses apply to a slightly different subset of cases than earlier analyses,

TABLE 5–2:
Explanatory Models of Hourly Wage

	Dependent Variable					
	Natural Logarithm of Annual Earnings, 1976 (N = 1,483) Metric Regression Coefficients (standard error in parentheses)					
Independent Variables	Marital History Variables	Correction for selection bias	Labor Market Segmentation Variables	Human Capital Variables	Structural Model	Individualist Model
	[1]	[2]	[3]	[4]	[5]	[6]
Nonwhite	−.14***	−.27***	−.10***	−.04	−.03	−.05*
	(.03)	(.02)	(.02)	(.02)	(.02)	(.03)
Marital History Variables						
Recently divorced[a]	.08*	.03	.00	.00	.01	.03
	(.05)	(.04)	(.04)	(.03)	(.04)	(.04)
Long-term divorced[a]	.17***	.10*	.07*	.05	.07*	.10**
	(.05)	(.05)	(.04)	(.04)	(.04)	(.04)
Never married	.22***	.05	.02	.00	.02	.05
	(.05)	(.05)	(.04)	(.04)	(.04)	(.05)
Other marital history[b]	−.05	−.03	−.02	−.02	−.02	−.01
	(.03)	(.02)	(.02)	(.02)	(.02)	(.02)
Correction for selection bias		1.83***	.99***	.16	.13	.18
		(.10)	(.10)	(.14)	(.14)	(.15)
Labor Market Segmentation Variables						
Job characteristics:						
(a) Decision latitude			.01***		.003*	.003*
			(.001)		(.001)	(.001)
(b) Union membership			.18***		.11***	.11***
			(.02)		(.02)	(.02)
(c) Job insecurity			−.20***		−.08	−.08
			(.06)		(.06)	(.06)
(d) Supervisory status			.18***		.12*	.12*
			(.06)		(.06)	(.06)
Firm size (Ln)			.06***		.04***	.04***
			(.005)		(.005)	(.005)
Core industry			.22***		.18***	.18***
			(.02)		(.02)	(.02)

[a] Differences between the coefficients for the long-term divorced and the recently divorced are statistically significant in equations [1], [3] and [6] at p < .10.

[b] Two-tailed significance test.

(Continued on next page)

TABLE 5–2—*Continued*

	Dependent Variable					
	Natural Logarithm of Annual Earnings, 1976 (N = 1,483) Metric Regression Coefficients (standard error in parentheses)					
Independent Variables	Marital History Variables	Correction for selection bias	Labor Market Segmentation Variables	Human Capital Variables	Structural Model	Individualist Model
	[1]	[2]	[3]	[4]	[5]	[6]
Human Capital Variables						
Education				.03***	.03***	.02***
				(.01)	(.01)	(.01)
Education, squared				—	—	—
Years of work experience				.02***	.01***	.02***
				(.005)	(.005)	(.005)
Years of work experience, squared				−.0002*	−.0002	−.0003**
				(.0001)	(.0001)	(.0001)
Years at current job				.02***	.02***	.02***
				(.004)	(.004)	(.004)
Years at current job, squared				−.0003*	−.0003*	−.0003*
				(.0002)	(.0002)	(.0002)
Received occupational training				.04*	.04*	.06**
				(.02)	(.02)	(.02)
Occupational status				.01***	.01***	.01***
				(.001)	(.001)	(.001)
Family Role Variables						
Any other earners in household					—	—
Earnings of other household members (Ln)					.003	.003
					(.002)	(.003)
Egalitarian gender attitudes					.01**	.01***
					(.003)	(.003)
Any children					—	—
Number of children					—	—
Total fertility					—	—
Age					—	—
Age, squared					—	—
R^2	.05***	.22***	.43***	.52***	.52***	.44***
Change in R^2	NA	.17***	.21***	.11***	.004***	−.08***

Ln = Natural logarithm transformation.

— = Variable considered for entry into equation, but did not meet significance level criterion (p<.05).

* p < .05

** p < .01

*** p < .001

which focused on employment activity (labor force status, hours, earnings) throughout 1976. Wage data for 1977 rather than 1976 are used because they are subject to less error than a measure of average annual wages.[2]

Never-married women and both groups of divorced women have significantly higher wages than married women, after controlling for the effects of race (see Table 5-2, column [1]). The effect for recently divorced women is weak—only about 8%. However, long-term divorced women have an hourly wage 17% higher than married women; the corresponding figure for never-married women is 22%. While these effects may seem relatively small, it should be noted that the effect of race is of roughly the same magnitude. By this standard, these two marital history differences are at least as important as racial differences in hourly wage. The difference in magnitude of the coefficients for the recently divorced and the long-term divorced suggests that the wage advantage of divorced women increases over time. This finding is consistent with the findings from the time series data presented in Chapter 3. It is also consistent with an analysis predicting 1977 hourly wage from the number of years since divorce, which indicates that wages are higher among women who have been divorced longer (data not shown). These findings suggest that adjustments to divorce have stronger effects on women's wages over the long term.

When the correction for selection bias is added to the model (Table 5-2, column [2]), the wage advantages of recently divorced and never-married women are reduced, to 3% and 5%, respectively. However, the wage advantage of the long-term divorced remains statistically significant (10%). This finding suggests that even after controlling for background factors predisposing divorced women to work, divorce causes changes which, in the long run, increase women's wages.

The differences in wages among marital history categories indicate that marriage reduces wage attainment of women. Divorce seems to result in changes which, over time, increase wages again. While most previous research found no difference between divorced and married women with respect to hourly wage, the results here do indicate a wage advantage for long-term divorced women. Although the marital history variables account for only a small portion of the variation in wages, it is the theoretical importance rather than the statistical power of this model that is of interest.

5.4 EXPLANATORY MODELS OF HOURLY WAGE

After labor market segmentation variables are added to the wage equation (Table 5-2, column [3]), the difference between the long-term divorced and the continuously married declines by about 3 percentage points.

Most of this reduction is due to the addition of firm size to the model. As noted in the findings regarding annual earnings, long-term divorced women tend to work in larger firms than married women.

When the human capital variables are added to the model (Table 5-2, column [4]), the wage advantage for the long-term divorced is reduced further (from 7% to 5%), and is no longer statistically significant. This reduction is achieved primarily because long-term divorced women have more years of work experience. To elaborate on this finding, other dimensions of work history and labor supply were substituted for work experience (data not shown). Withdrawals of respondents from the labor force during the 10 years of the study period had a negative effect on wages, but did not account for the wage advantage of long-term divorced woman. Working full-time rather than part-time had a positive effect on wages,[3] but did not reduce the wage advantage of long-term divorced women. Apparently, this wage advantage can be partially explained by differences in years of work experience, but not by differences in the number of labor force withdrawals or in the proportion of women working part-time.

The addition of family role variables to the model (Table 5-2, column [5]) has minimal impact on wage differences among women due to marital history. To the extent that there is an effect, the wage advantages of divorced and never-married women increase a bit. These increases in the effects of the marital history variables are due to the addition of the variable "earnings of other household members" to the equation. The wage advantage of long-term divorced women becomes statistically significant, but is still relatively small, 7%. None of the other family role variables has any appreciable impact on the marital history effects.

The small unexplained portion of the wage advantage of long-term divorced women may be attributable to their greater ability to receive higher returns than married women do for one or more of the demand factors, to maximize returns on their human capital, or to minimize the effects of their family roles on their work behavior. To test these possibilities, interaction terms were created to allow the effect of each variable in the model to vary by marital history (data not shown). Returns to variables in the model are the same for married and divorced women. Never-married women have higher returns to firm size, suggesting that they may be favored over married women in large firms. Tests of interactions between race and all other variables in the model indicate that two are significant (data not shown): nonwhite women have lower returns for decision latitude and higher returns for education than do whites.[4] Controlling for these differences in returns does not change the marital history effects.

To provide a comparison with the structural model, the "pure" individualist model of hourly wages was estimated (Table 5-2, column [6]).

As in the case of hours and of earnings, the structural model explains more variance than the individualist model (52% vs. 44%). Furthermore, the individualist model is slightly less effective than the structural model in accounting for marital history differences.

5.5 DISCUSSION OF FINDINGS ON PERSONAL INCOME

While marriage reduces women's annual earnings (compare the earnings of married and never-married women), divorce increases annual earnings, especially after a long period. Long-term divorced women, but not recently divorced women or never-married women, also have a significant hourly wage advantage over married women. This finding suggests that the earnings advantage of never-married and recently divorced women is due primarily to the greater number of hours they work; the earnings advantage of long-term divorced women is due both to their greater hours worked *and* to their higher hourly wage. The findings from the wage model support the argument that divorce results in work adjustments which have a positive long-run effect on earning power.

Surprisingly, some of the adjustments to divorce are apparently made by employers. Long-term divorced women are more likely than married women to work in larger firms. Never-married women are hired for jobs with greater decision latitude than are married women, and are more likely to work in large firms. Never-married women also have higher wage returns for firm size than do married women. The importance of firm size indicates that large firms offer single women greater opportunities than married women. In a part of the labor market where women have greater opportunity (i.e., large firms), single women (i.e., divorced and never-married women) are more likely to be hired than married women. Employers who provide better opportunities for women apparently prefer to hire and retain single women rather than married women, perhaps because they view them as more stable or committed employees.[5]

One interpretation of these results is that employers' perceptions of marital history are as important as the actual effects of marital history on a woman's human capital. On average, employers prefer never-married and divorced women as employees, especially those whom they regard as unlikely to marry or remarry. One indicator that a woman is unlikely to marry or remarry is her long-term status as a single woman. To carry this reasoning a step further, there is evidence of discrimination by marital status in the labor market. Never-married women have more desirable jobs than other women, which may reflect the effects of promotions in an internal labor market. Divorced and never-married women are more likely to be employed in large firms and in core industries than other women, which probably reflects the effects of hiring practices. More never-married women and divorced women appear to be recruited than other women in jobs, firms, and industries that can afford to pay more.

To elaborate on this finding, a model was developed to test whether a preference for single women exists within the most advantaged labor market segments. If employers prefer single women, that preference is expected to be reflected more strongly in larger firms, where career ladders and promotions are more common and wages are higher. Large firms are more able than small firms to act on preferences that cost money. In small firms, where promotion opportunities are more limited and profits are lower, employers are less able to give employees promotions or higher wages.

To test this hypothesis, marital history effects on hourly wage were estimated separately for small, medium, and large firms (see Table 5-3).[6] The wage advantages of divorced and never-married women generally increase with firm size (Table 5-3, Section I).[7] (The major exception to this pattern is that long-term divorced women fare better in small than in medium-sized firms. However, neither coefficient is statistically significant).

An alternative explanation for these findings could be derived from human capital theory: variation in women's work history, not employer preferences, may account for these differences by marital history. Marital history may not affect wages in small firms, if women choose these firms because they allow flexible work patterns. In large firms, married women may perform more poorly because of the constraints of family roles. For example, married women might be less likely than other women to have continuous work histories or long job tenure, which would penalize them, relative to single women, in large firms. In small firms, intermittent work patterns are more common and are more easily accommodated.

While these human capital arguments would account for the findings, they are not supported by the data (see Table 5-3, Section II). After controlling for human capital variables (education, experience, tenure in job), the differences in patterns of marital history effects by firm size are weaker, but still generally consistent with the hypothesis that single women are preferred over married women in large firms. These findings do not resolve the question of whether it is employer preferences or work history that accounts for the effects of women's marital history. However, they do suggest (1) that human capital explanations cannot easily account for these effects, and (2) that an employer preference for divorced and never-married women is a plausible explanation for these effects, and ought to be investigated further. These results illustrate the importance of considering the effect of marital history on the behavior of both employees and employers. Research is needed on employers' hiring and promotion practices to

TABLE 5–3:

Effects of Marital History on Women's Hourly Wage, by Size of Firm

	Dependent Variable		
	Natural Logarithm of Hourly Wage, 1977 Metric Regression Coefficients (standard error in parentheses)		
		SIZE OF FIRM	
Marital History	Small (2–24 employees)	Medium (25–499 employees)	Large (500 or more employees)
Section I: Marital History[a]			
Recently divorced	−.03	.04	.07
	(.10)	(.08)	(.06)
Long-term divorced	.14	.05	.15**
	(.11)	(.07)	(.07)
Never married	−.10	.12	.32***
	(.12)	(.08)	(.07)
(Number)	(416)	(520)	(547)
Section II: Marital History[b]			
Recently divorced	−.04	.05	.00
	(.09)	(.06)	(.05)
Long-term divorced	.03	.04	.09*
	(.10)	(.06)	(.06)
Never married	−.26	−.04	.14**
	(.11)	(.07)	(.06)
(Number)	(416)	(520)	(547)

[a] The excluded (reference) category is continuously married women. These equations control for race and "other" marital history (effects not shown).

[b] The excluded (reference) category is continuously married women. In addition to race and "other" marital history, these equations also control for education, years of work experience, years at current job, and the correction for selection bias (effects not shown).

  * $p < .05$
  ** $p < .01$
  *** $p < .001$

determine whether and how employers differentiate between married and single women.

From a human capital/family role perspective, the earnings and wage disadvantage of married women is due to the work disincentives associated with having a spouse, and to the time married women spend out of the labor force for child care. The importance of work experience over the long-term illustrates the significance and shortcomings of prior research that focused on the short-term effects of divorce on labor supply. Divorced and never-married women are more likely to work and to work more hours per year, and are less likely to withdraw from the labor force, than married women. This pattern was consistently found in prior research, and was confirmed in models predicting labor supply in Chapter 4. However, since the effects of work experience and labor force withdrawals on wages accumulate over time, the effects of increased labor supply on earnings and wages can be observed only after a sufficiently long period.

The family role variables did not account for the marital history effects, but strengthened them. While the reasons for this finding have been discussed, perhaps a recapitulation should be presented here. Women who have high earning potential are likely to be married to men who also have high earning potential. Married women who have high earning potential (as measured, for example, by education) are less likely to work; however, if they do work, they work because they have found jobs paying above their high reservation wage. Well-educated divorced and never-married women are more likely to work than married women, which accounts for a portion of their earnings and wage advantage over married women. However, considering that the reservation wage of divorced and never-married women is not raised by earnings of a spouse, their advantage relative to married women is higher than would be expected.

While it may seem surprising that controlling for the presence of children does not affect earnings or wages, recall that these are net effects, after controlling for labor market segmentation and human capital variables. The negative effects of children on women's earnings and wages are mediated by their effects on human capital. Since the indirect effects of children are of considerable interest, more detailed analyses were conducted. About 56% of married and 55% of recently divorced women had children in the household in 1977, compared with only 31% of the long-term divorced. The finding that long-term divorced women are much less likely to have children than married women could account for the gross earnings and wage advantages of long-term divorced women over married women observed (see Tables 5-1 and 5-2, column [2]).[8] To test this possibility, the gross effects were recomputed separately for women who had children and women who did not (data not shown). The earnings advantage of recently divorced and long-term divorced women is as strong among those who have children as among those who don't. The wage advantage is actually stronger among those who have children than among those who don't. Furthermore, the mean earnings and wages of divorced women who have children and those who do not have children are virtually the same. These findings provide further evidence that, for divorced women, children provide an economic incentive to work.[9] However, divorced women who have children have a lower standard of living than those who have no children in the household, since they are supporting a larger family on the same amount of income (see discussion in Chapter 6).

Family responsibilities affect married and divorced women differently. While married women who have children invest more time in child care and less in work, divorced women who have children invest more time in work to support their children, and make alternate arrangements for child care. Unfortunately, questions on time spent caring for children were not asked in the 1977 NLS. However, data on type of child care arrangements are available. While 30% of married working women in this sample rely on their spouses for child care, divorced women rely heavily on their older children and other relatives for child care.

These analyses of the differential effects of children for married and divorced women provide a better understanding of the economic trade-offs these women make. While results presented in Chapter 3 indicate that women in this cohort make trade-offs between their own earnings and spouse's income, they also make trade-offs regarding child-care arrangements. Many married women stay at home to care for their children, and many married women who work rely on their spouses for child care. Divorced women cannot rely on a spouse, and most cannot afford to stay home. Therefore, alternative arrangements must be made. As a result of divorce, women who have children experience both increased financial need (to support themselves and their children), *and* in many cases, the loss of their source of child care (either their spouses or themselves). In spite of the loss of child care, most divorced women who have children respond to financial need by working. The need to provide economic support for children prompts some divorced women to seek alternative child care arrangements.

Divorced women who have children are as able to increase their earnings as those who do not. It is not clear whether this finding is consistent or inconsistent with human capital theory. On the one hand, children increase economic need, and divorced women who have children would be expected to maximize earnings to support their children. On the other hand, children increase household responsibilities that might interfere with work, and divorced women who have children would be expected to have a difficult time increasing their earning capacity. Human capital theory does not provide clear guidance on this issue.

The explanatory models of earnings and wages perform much better in accounting for the advantage of never-married women than of either group of divorced women. The differential ability of the models to account for the wage advantages of divorced and never-married women may reflect differences between unplanned and planned careers. The advantage of never-married women, whose careers are more planned, is reflected in the standard measures of human capital and of demand for labor. However, at the time most divorced women made their marriage and work plans, they did not expect to rely solely on their own earnings for support. Presumably, their work plans changed significantly in response to the prospect of divorce, originally an unexpected event. Divorced women may make subtle adjustments in their orientation to work; the effects of these adjustments may not be captured by the individual characteristics measured here. Or employers, believing that long-term divorced women are less likely to remarry, may favor such women in ways not reflected in the measures of demand considered here.

While a synthesis of findings and their significance will be presented in Chapter 7, one final issue should be briefly addressed here. Results presented in Chapters 4 and 5 provide an empirical test of the adequacy of the individualist and structural theories in accounting for women's wages, hours, and earnings.[10] In each case, the structural model explains more variance than the individualist model, indicating that labor market segmentation variables significantly improve the explanatory power of the model of labor market outcomes. Furthermore, the structural model accounts for a greater portion of the marital history differences than the individualist model with respect to earnings and wages (although not hours). These results support the argument that both individual factors and labor market segmentation affect labor market outcomes.

CHAPTER 6

Determinants of Economic Well-Being Among Divorced Women

6.1 INTRODUCTION: DEVELOPMENT OF A LIFE-COURSE MODEL

Thus far, this study has considered the economic effects of divorce by comparing divorced women to married women. This chapter considers how the effects of divorce on economic well-being depend on women's life history prior to divorce. Focusing only on divorced women, this chapter develops an explanatory model based on the life-course perspective.[1] A divorced woman's work and family history, both before and after divorce, is hypothesized to affect her standard of living. This life-course model is tested on several measures of economic well-being: income/needs ratio, poverty status and public assistance status.

Lopata and Norr (1980) have suggested that a woman's prior orientation to work at home and in the labor market has a significant impact on how she copes with economic need after divorce. Women whose primary role has been that of homemaker have difficulty finding "jobs that will adequately support them and their dependents."[2] On the other hand, career women, who have had a steady attachment to the work force, are better prepared to support themselves. Women who have worked intermittently, perhaps leaving the labor force for several years to raise children, are more likely to have a job, or to find work, than those who were full-time homemakers. However, intermittent workers would be expected to earn less than career women, since they are more likely to be employed "in relatively low-paying female-dominated jobs."[3]

The importance of prior orientation to work in the labor market is similarly emphasized in lifetime labor supply models. These models suggest that individuals plan their lifetime labor supply pattern based on anticipated wages (planning to work more hours when wages are expected to be high), time preferences (deciding whether they prefer to work more hours now or in the future), and interest rates (planning to work more hours now so that earnings can be invested and labor supply reduced later in life). Hill and Stafford (1985) suggest that young women, through a sorting process, plan to focus either on household work or on work in the market. While it is not clear whether the extent of involvement in paid work affects fertility, or whether fertility affects decisions about paid work, this sorting process differentially positions women for a return to the labor market later in life.[4]

Lifetime labor supply models make an important distinction between anticipated and unanticipated changes in work plans.[5] Some women expect to move in and out of the labor force, and plan accordingly. For other women, a return to the labor force is unexpected; their early labor supply decisions were made without regard to such a return. (This description fits the pattern Lopata and Norr refer to as the "displaced homemaker".) For homemakers, divorce is likely to cause an unanticipated return to the labor market, representing a disequilibrium in their lifetime labor supply profile. For intermittent workers, a return to work is likely to have been anticipated (even had the women not divorced), although it may occur earlier than had been anticipated. For career women (who never planned to drop out of the labor force) and intermittent workers, earnings and economic well-being after divorce can be expected to be higher than for homemakers. Career women would be expected to fare better than intermittent workers since they presumably have accumulated more human capital.

While prior work history is important, women also respond to life events. Divorce may result in adjustments in work behavior. Evidence for this argument is provided in the analyses in previous chapters. Divorced women have a stronger attachment to the labor market than married women. Among divorced women, then, those who have more work experience at the time of their divorce are expected to have a higher standard of living after divorce. Other adaptations that might improve the earning power of divorced women include returning to school and/or seeking additional occupational training.

Divorce also involves changes in social context which may affect economic well-being. Divorced women who live with a working adult will generally have a higher standard of living (assuming they share income) than those who do not. Divorced women who have children are expected to fare worse than those who do not, for two reasons. First, children represent an additional expense, increasing economic need. Second, the constraints of child care may limit a divorced woman's work options with respect to hours of work and location of job. Women who receive alimony and/or child support are predicted to be better off financially than those who do not. In summary, the life-course model suggests that prior work orientation, post-divorce changes in work orientation, and post-divorce social context are expected to account for variation in economic well-being among divorced women.

Some predictions of the life-course model are also consistent with those of lifetime labor supply models. Both models predict that economic well-being after divorce depends on prior work orientation and on post-divorce changes in work orientation.

The analyses of income/needs ratio, poverty status, and public assistance status were conducted using data for all women in the NLS who were divorced for the first time between 1967 and 1977 and who were still divorced in 1977. Information about date of divorce is combined with data from intermediate surveys to create measures of pre-divorce and post-divorce characteristics. The model is tested in the following manner: First, race and age are entered as control variables. Race is retained in each model, whether or not it is statistically significant, to control for the effects of the oversampling of blacks (see discussion in Chapter 4).[6] Next, three sets of explanatory variables are introduced sequentially: pre-divorce characteristics, post-divorce characteristics, and post-divorce social context variables.

The pre-divorce characteristics include work orientation, education, and occupational training. Pre-divorce work orientation is measured using two dummy variables, based on a description of life patterns by Lopata and Norr (1980). Women are coded as "homemakers" if they worked less than 20% of the years between leaving school and the time of their divorce, and as "career" women if they worked over 80% of those years. The excluded reference category, intermittent workers, includes women who worked between 20% and 80% of those years.

Measures of post-divorce characteristics include years of work experience after divorce,[7] whether the woman received occupational training after divorce, and the woman's 1977 gender attitudes. (Post-divorce schooling would also have been included here, but none of the divorced women in this sample returned to school.)

Post-divorce social context is measured using the following variables: presence of other adults in the household in 1977 who worked in the previous year, the number of hours worked by other adults in the previous year, the presence and number of children in the household, total fertility, whether any alimony was received, whether any child support was received, and the amount of alimony and of child support payments.

6.2 EXPLANATORY MODEL OF INCOME/NEEDS RATIO

The first measure of economic well-being considered here is the income/needs ratio. Chapter 3 defined "need" to be the family's poverty threshold, as determined by the Census Bureau, based on the number of family members. The income/needs ratio, unlike family income, is a measure that takes into account differences in family size among divorced women. The model developed here controls for race; age was tested as a control variable, but had no significant effect, and was dropped from the model.[8]

Pre-divorce work experience is an important determinant of economic well-being for these divorced women (Table 6–1, column [1]). Women who were homemakers have a lower standard of living than intermittent workers. Surprisingly, however, career women do not fare significantly better than intermittent workers.

Even after controlling for these work experience variables, every additional year of education increases the income/needs ratio by 15%. Well-educated women, even those who were homemakers, fare better after divorce. This finding is consistent with research by Appelbaum (1981) who found a positive effect of education on hourly wage for married homemakers returning to the labor force. However, the results presented here also indicate that regardless of their level of education, homemakers do not fare as well as other women. Women who stayed home to raise children are at the greatest disadvantage after divorce. These findings at least partially support the argument that the economic effects of divorce depend on a woman's pre-divorce work characteristics. A woman's education and her work history during marriage are important predictors of her economic security in the event of divorce. These pre-divorce characteristics account for about one-fourth of the variation in women's economic well-being after divorce.

Seen from a life-course perspective, these findings indicate the importance of being able to draw on life experience in responding to the economic consequences of divorce. Women who did not expect to return to work invested less in human capital and had discontinuous work histories as a result. Women who became homemakers had less education than intermittent workers or career women (10.8 years vs. 11.4 and 13.2 years, respectively). When an unexpected event such as divorce occurred, homemakers were poorly prepared to find a well-paying job. Intermittent workers and those who worked continuously while married were better prepared to support themselves. These findings reflect the importance of early decisions about investment in human capital.

A woman's years of work experience after divorce have a positive effect on her standard of living (Table 6-1, column [2]). Egalitarian gender attitudes also have a positive effect on economic well-being, perhaps because they reflect variation in how women respond to their work situation. Controlling for post-divorce characteristics does not reduce the negative effect of having been a homemaker. This finding indicates two things. First, homemakers have less work experience than other women after divorce. On average, women who were homemakers worked 36% of the years after divorce, versus 55% for intermittent workers and 56% for career women.

TABLE 6–1:

Explanatory Model of Income/Needs Ratio among Divorced Women

Independent Variables	Dependent Variable		
	Natural Logarithm of Income/Needs Ratio, 1976 (N = 117) Metric Regression Coefficients (standard error in parentheses)		
	Pre-Divorce Variables	Post-Divorce Variables	Social Context Variables
	[1]	[2]	[3]
Background Variables			
Nonwhite	− .00	− .04	− .05
	(.20)	(.20)	(.19)
Age	—	—	—
Pre-Divorce Characteristics			
Homemaker	− .64***	− .62**	− .56**
	(.22)	(.22)	(.21)
Career woman	.09	.16	.13
	(.23)	(.22)	(.22)
Education, 1967	.15***	.11***	.12***
	(.03)	(.03)	(.03)
Received occupational training	—	—	—
Post-Divorce Characteristics			
Work experience		.08*	.08*
		(.04)	(.04)
Received occupational training		—	—
Egalitarian gender attitudes, 1977		.07**	.07***
		(.02)	(.02)
Social Context			
Any other earners in household, 1976			—
Hours worked by other household members, 1976			—
Any children, 1977			− .35**
			(.16)
Number of children, 1977			—
Total fertility, 1977			—
Any alimony received, 1976			—

(Continued on next page)

TABLE 6–1—*Continued*

	Dependent Variable		
	Natural Logarithm of Income/Needs Ratio, 1976 (N = 117) Metric Regression Coefficients (standard error in parentheses)		
Independent Variables	Pre-Divorce Variables	Post-Divorce Variables	Social Context Variables
	[1]	[2]	[3]
Amount of alimony received, 1976			—
Any child support received, 1976			—
Amount of child support received, 1976			—
R^2	.26***	.32***	.35***
Change in R^2	NA	.06***	.03**

— = Variable considered for entry into equation, but did not meet significance level criterion (p < .05).

  * p < .05
 ** p < .01
*** p < .001

Furthermore, among those who have equal amounts of experience after divorce, negative effects of having been a homemaker remain. Post-divorce work adjustments are more difficult for homemakers, and are less effective.

Among the social context variables (Table 6-1, column [3]), the presence of children has a significant negative effect as expected, since children increase economic need without increasing income. Having other adult workers in the household has no effect on the income/needs ratio, since other workers increase both income and need. The findings regarding the effects of other social context variables are interesting because they reveal that none of these variables have an effect on economic well-being.

Surprisingly, divorced women who receive alimony and/or child support have no financial advantage over women who do not.[9] There are at least three possible explanations for this finding. Alimony and child support may be a primary source of income for women who receive it, rather than a supplement to work or public assistance income. Or, alimony and child support payments may supplement other income, but are too small to improve the income/needs ratio significantly.[10] A third possibility is that alimony and child support payments are substantial, but only divorced women who have otherwise low incomes receive such payments. Data from the NLS give more credence to the last explanation than to the first two. Among the 18 divorced women who received alimony in 1976, 78% also had earnings, while among the 50 divorced women who received child support, 86% had earned income.[11] Earnings accounted for about 61% of family income among those receiving alimony and 68% among those receiving child support. Alimony and child support, therefore, do not appear to be an alternative to working. Nor are these payments an insignificant portion of income. Among divorced women who received alimony, such payments accounted for 22% of their mean $10,900 1976 income, improving their income/needs ratio from 2.0 to 2.5. Women receiving child support payments derived 24% of their mean $10,700 1976 income from that source, which improved their income/needs ratio from 2.0 to 2.3. While these payments are not the primary source of support for most of these divorced women, these women would have a significantly lower standard of living without such payments. Alimony and child support payments, while small, increase their family income to a level about equal to that of other divorced women who do not receive such payments.

6.3 EXPLANATORY MODEL OF POVERTY STATUS

This section considers how pre-divorce characteristics and post-divorce adjustments and social context affect poverty status for recently divorced women. The factors that determine poverty status may not be the same as those determining income/needs ratio, since the former is concerned with the lower end of the distribution, while the latter measures economic well-being over the whole range of the income distribution. The model developed here identifies the variables that predict whether women experience extreme economic deprivation after divorce.

About 19% of the divorced women considered in this analysis were poor in 1977. (Poverty status is defined here as a dichotomous variable—coded 0 if the income/needs ratio exceeds 1.0, coded 1 otherwise.) Logistic regression is used to estimate a model for this dichotomous dependent variable.[12] Race is retained in this model as a control variable, although its effect is not statistically significant (Table 6-2, column [1]).

Women who were homemakers prior to divorce have a greater chance of being poor than intermittent workers. Career women, however, are no less likely than intermittent workers to be poor after divorce. This pattern is similar to that found for the income/needs ratio. Apparently, divorced women who have at least some work experience are able to capitalize on it to avoid poverty, regardless of whether they worked continuously or intermittently. As expected, women who have more years of education are less likely to be poor after divorce.

TABLE 6–2:
Explanatory Model of Poverty Status among Divorced Women

	Dependent Variable		
	Poverty Status, 1976 (N = 117) Logistic Regression Coefficients (standard error in parentheses)		
Independent Variables	Pre-Divorce Variables	Post-Divorce Variables	Social Context Variables
	[1]	[2]	[3]
Background Variables			
Nonwhite	.32	.75	.92
	(.61)	(.69)	(.72)
Age	—	—	—
Pre-Divorce Characteristics			
Homemaker	1.24*	1.38*	1.32*
	(.61)	(.67)	(.71)
Career woman	.16	−.52	−.40
	(.79)	(.96)	(.98)
Education, 1967	−.31**	−.13	−.15
	(.11)	(.12)	(.13)
Received occupational training	—	—	—
Post-Divorce Characteristics			
Work experience		−.41**	−.47**
		(.19)	(.21)
Received occupational training		—	—
Egalitarian gender attitudes, 1977		−.26***	−.33***
		(.08)	(.10)
Social Context			
Any other earners in household, 1976			—
Hours worked by other household members, 1976			—
Any children, 1977			1.46*
			(.68)
Number of children, 1977			—
Total fertility, 1977			—
Any alimony received, 1976			—
Amount of alimony received, 1976			—

(Continued on next page)

TABLE 6–2—*Continued*

	Dependent Variable		
	Poverty Status, 1976 (N = 117) Logistic Regression Coefficients (standard error in parentheses)		
Independent Variables	Pre-Divorce Variables	Post-Divorce Variables	Social Context Variables
	[1]	[2]	[3]
Any child support received, 1976			—
Amount of child support received, 1976			—
Chi-square	15.30***	27.76***	33.04***
Degrees of freedom	(4)	(6)	(7)
Change in chi-square	NA	12.46***	5.28*

— = Variable considered for entry into equation, but did not meet significance level criterion (p < .05).
 * p < .05
 ** p < .01
 *** p < .001

Adding measures of post-divorce work orientation significantly increases the predictive ability of the model (Table 6-2, column [2]). Women who have more years of work experience after divorce, and women who have egalitarian gender attitudes are less likely than other divorced women to be poor, after controlling for prior work orientation. Introducing the post-divorce characteristics reduces the effect of education to a statistically insignificant level (compare Table 6-2, columns [1] and [2]). This finding indicates that education reduces the likelihood of poverty for divorced women through its effect on post-divorce characteristics. Specifically, women who have more years of education are also likely to have more recent work experience and egalitarian gender attitudes, and so are less likely to be poor. Post-divorce characteristics do not account for the increased likelihood of poverty among homemakers. Even after controlling for recent work experience and gender attitudes, divorced homemakers are still more likely than intermittent workers to be poor. Post-divorce adjustments are less effective in avoiding poverty for homemakers than for other women, a finding consistent with both the life-course perspective and the lifetime labor supply model.

Among the social context variables (Table 6-2, column [3]), the presence of other adult workers did not reduce a divorced woman's chances of being poor. Women who have children are more likely than other women to be poor after divorce, even after controlling for the effects of education, training, recent work experience, and gender attitudes. Receiving alimony and/or child support payments did not reduce a divorced woman's chances of being poor. As noted earlier, these payments are generally received by divorced women who have lower income from other sources. This finding suggests that alimony and child support payments are inadequate, since a presumed goal of such payments is the avoidance of economic deprivation for the divorced woman and her children.

6.4 EXPLANATORY MODEL OF PUBLIC ASSISTANCE STATUS

The third and final model of economic well-being considers whether life history and current social context account for a divorced woman's public assistance status. There is only a moderate relationship between poverty status and public assistance status (lambda = .11). About 38% of poor divorced women do not receive public assistance, while 35% of divorced women on public assistance are not poor.[13] Furthermore, the factors which determine public assistance status may be different from those which determine poverty status. About 12% of the divorced women considered in this analysis received public assistance in 1976. Results for the logistic regression model (Table 6-3, column [1]) show that nonwhite divorced women are more likely to receive public assistance. Age also has a significant effect: older divorced women are more likely to receive public assistance than younger divorced women.

Only one of the pre-divorce variables has a statistically significant effect on the likelihood of a divorced woman receiving public assistance. Being a homemaker increases the chances of receiving public assistance, while career women are no less likely to receive public assistance than intermittent workers. Married women who stay home to raise children are at a much greater risk of having to rely on public assistance after divorce. Surprisingly, education has no statistically significant effect on divorced women's public assistance status. Highly educated women are as likely as women who have fewer years of education to receive public assistance after divorce (controlling for the effects of race, age, and work experience).

Controlling for post-divorce characteristics significantly improves the predictive ability of the model (Table 6-3, column [2]). Divorced women who have more recent work experience and women who have egalitarian gender attitudes are less likely to be on public assistance. These findings parallel those of previous models.

TABLE 6–3:
Explanatory Model of Public Assistance Status among Divorced Women

Independent Variables	Dependent Variable		
	Public Assistance Status, 1976 (N = 117) Logistic Regression Coefficients (standard error in parentheses)		
	Pre-Divorce Variables	Post-Divorce Variables	Social Context Variables
	[1]	[2]	[3]
Background Variables			
Nonwhite	1.95**	2.76***	3.01***
	(.73)	(.93)	(.96)
Age	.21**	.20*	.25**
	(.09)	(.10)	(.11)
Pre-Divorce Characteristics			
Homemaker	1.22*	1.36	.86
	(.76)	(.86)	(.92)
Career woman	−.51	−1.21	−1.67
	(.98)	(1.17)	(1.26)
Education, 1967	−.19	.04	.06
	(.13)	(.15)	(.15)
Received occupational training	—	—	—
Post-Divorce Characteristics			
Work experience		−.41*	−.52*
		(.23)	(.25)
Received occupational training		—	—
Egalitarian gender attitudes, 1977		−.32**	−.39***
		(.11)	(.13)
Social Context			
Any other earners in household, 1976			—
Hours worked by other household members, 1976			—
Any children, 1977			1.78*
			(.93)
Number of children, 1977			—
Total fertility, 1977			—
Any alimony received, 1976			—
Amount of alimony received, 1976			—
Any child support received, 1976			—

(Continued on next page)

TABLE 6–3—*Continued*

	Dependent Variable		
	Public Assistance Status, 1976 (N = 117) Logistic Regression Coefficients (standard error in parentheses)		
Independent Variables	Pre-Divorce Variables	Post-Divorce Variables	Social Context Variables
	[1]	[2]	[3]
Amount of child support received, 1976			—
Chi-square	25.08***	36.19***	40.53***
Degrees of freedom	(5)	(7)	(8)
Change in chi-square	NA	11.11***	4.34*

— = Variable considered for entry into equation, but did not meet significance level
    criterion (p < .05).
  * p < .05
 ** p < .01
*** p < .001

Having children in the household is generally a requirement for receiving public assistance, and this variable is therefore not strictly exogenous. It is not surprising that divorced women who have children in the household were more likely than other divorced women to receive public assistance (Table 6-3, column [3]). It is interesting, however, that controlling for the presence of children substantially reduces the coefficient for divorced homemakers. This finding indicates that one of the reasons divorced homemakers are more likely than other divorced women to receive public assistance is that they are more likely to have children in the household. Surprisingly, presence of another adult earner does not reduce the likelihood of receiving public assistance, even though it would be expected to make women less likely to be eligible for public assistance. Alimony and child support do not reduce the chances of receiving public assistance, presumably, as noted previously, because women receiving such payments have lower income from other sources.

6.5   DISCUSSION OF FINDINGS ON ECONOMIC WELL-BEING

The effects of divorce on women's economic well-being depend on a number of factors. Pre-divorce characteristics have a strong impact on all three measures of economic well-being. Women who maintain some attachment to the labor market while married are better able to make work adjustments after divorce and to avoid severe economic deprivation. Women who were homemakers are those most adversely affected by divorce. Homemakers have a lower income/needs ratio (1.5 vs. 2.6), a higher poverty rate (43% vs. 15%), and a higher rate of receiving public assistance (30% vs. 10%) than other divorced women. Intermittent workers and career women fare better than homemakers; however, career women generally fare no better than intermittent workers. Women who have at least some work experience are able to avoid severe economic deprivation whether they worked continuously or intermittently. The hypothesis that career women would fare better than intermittent workers is not supported by these data.

Post-divorce characteristics also affect economic well-being. This finding is consistent with the findings in previous chapters. Women increase their labor supply after divorce to compensate for loss of spouses' income. In spite of these adjustments, homemakers have a lower standard of living after divorce than other women, perhaps because they have less work experience after divorce than other women (1.4 vs. 2.3 years, on average). This finding suggests that post-divorce adjustments depend on pre-divorce work characteristics.

The only significant social context variable in any of the models is the presence of children, which is negatively associated with economic well-being. This effect is presumably due to the additional costs of raising children. Although divorced women who have children earn as much as those who do not have children (see discussion in Chapter 5), their economic need is greater since they have larger families. The work orientation or work opportunities of women who have children may also be different in ways not measured here. Homemakers are more likely to have children in the household than other divorced women (71% vs. 53%), which partially accounts for their lower standard of living. Children not only require large investments of time, but also interfere with the accumulation of human capital. Hill and Stafford (1985), arguing from a lifetime labor supply perspective, suggest that women tend to have either paid work or children as their major orientation, and invest in human capital accordingly. Findings from the NLS data are consistent with this view: women who adopted the role of full-time mother while married are those whose financial situation is most negatively affected by divorce.

Interestingly, alimony and child support do not improve economic well-being, once pre-divorce and post-divorce characteristics are controlled for. Alimony and child support are awarded to those divorced women who have the lowest earnings. While alimony and child support payments provide a significant proportion of family income for women who receive them (20–25%), earnings from work are the main source of income in these households. This finding suggests that alimony and child support are targeted toward some of the neediest divorced women. Nonetheless, the laws awarding alimony and child support payments, and the procedures enforcing collection of the awards, are inadequate. Clearly, many divorced women are poor in spite of such payments and must rely on public assistance.[14] If alimony and child support were ordered more often by the courts, if awards were sufficiently high, and if payment was enforced, fewer divorced women would be poor or need to depend on public assistance. These findings are consistent with the view that shortcomings in the award and enforcement of alimony and child support payments lead to increased poverty and reliance on public assistance among divorced women.[15] Yet, for most divorced women, earnings are the major source of income, whether or not they receive alimony, child support, or public assistance.

From a theoretical standpoint, the analyses in this chapter have provided support for the life-course approach. Specifically, the importance of work orientation and of changes in work orientation has been established for models of economic well-being after divorce. The economic effects of divorce depend, at least in part, on a woman's prior life history. While the experience of divorce is common to all these women, the economic effects of divorce depend on the women's orientation to work and family roles while still married. Divorce also produces changes in work behavior, illustrating the importance of the link between family and work outcomes.

As illustrated at several points, the predictions of a lifetime labor supply model are sometimes consistent with those of the life-course model. The lifetime labor supply model stresses the importance of early choices regarding work and family, and views the effects of divorce in light of whether a return to the labor force was anticipated or unanticipated. The model, however, does not consider that early choices may change as a result of divorce. A re-evaluation may take place, and adjustments to divorce (i.e., investments in human capital) may depend on whether or not women expect to remain divorced. Divorced women may also find that they prefer working to staying home. The analyses in this chapter provide support for the view that divorce, an unexpected event, has unexpected effects on work careers and on long-term economic well-being. Both early decisions and post-divorce investments in human capital are important determinants of economic well-being.

Differences between the life-course model and the lifetime labor supply model, insofar as they are considered here, are differences about whether work careers are primarily affected by early plans or by situational factors that change over the life course. The lifetime labor supply model implies that women plan investments in human capital and act accordingly. The life-course model, on the other hand, views work orientation as a part of life history. Work orientation may not be planned at all, or actual work orientation may deviate from planned work orientation. A behavioral measure of work orientation, such as the one used here, is more appropriate for this analysis since it takes into account the effects of an unexpected event like divorce, which may change a woman's work orientation.

CHAPTER 7

Conclusion

Rising divorce rates have had a significant impact on American women over the last several decades. No longer can most women assume that marriage will last "forever." Since half of all marriages now end in divorce, most women who marry today must consider how they will support themselves (and their children) if they become divorced.

The economic consequences of divorce are not likely to be as severe today as they were for women even a decade ago. Work has become normative for young married women. Few plan to spend their lives as full-time homemakers, although young women continue to face the problems of gender inequality in the labor market, and a lack of day care. There are still many young women who plan to work intermittently to balance the demands of work and child care. Some young women will be in a better financial position than others in the event of divorce as a result of choices they make about work and family. This book has considered the economic consequences of divorce for women of an earlier generation, who faced a different set of choices and constraints. In spite of these differences between the cohorts, the experience of this earlier generation offers several important lessons about women's economic well-being after divorce.

The results presented in this book also have implications for theories of labor market outcomes and work-family linkages. The analyses provide evidence on the relative merits of individualist and structural theories of labor market outcomes. They also illustrate how women balance the demands of work and family over the life cycle.

This chapter first reviews these theoretical issues, and then discusses the implications of the results for understanding women's economic well-being after divorce.

7.1 INDIVIDUALIST AND STRUCTURAL EXPLANATIONS OF LABOR MARKET OUTCOMES

This study has explained the effects of divorce using individualist and structural models of labor market outcomes. The individualist model developed here extends the standard human capital model by including measures of family roles. This approach attempts to consider explicitly the constraints that family roles place on women's work careers. The focus has been not on how family roles affect accumulation of human capital, but on the direct effects of family roles on work outcomes, after controlling for the effects of human capital variables. The structural model developed here employs measures of segmentation at the level of the job, the firm, and the industry.[1] By considering several levels of analysis, the model measures a variety of structural effects ranging from unionization to the market power of the industry. While the models could be improved further (see later discussion), the analyses conducted here have compared results for well-developed models of each approach. Three important points of comparison can be considered: how the models account for variation in women's hours, earnings and wages, how the models account for the relationship between their wages and hours, and how the models account for racial differences in hours, earnings, and wages.

The results presented in Chapters 4 and 5 clearly support the argument that a structural model provides more explanatory power than a purely individualist model. The structural model accounted for more variance in hours, earnings, and wages than the individualist model. The structural model was also consistently better (although in some cases only slightly so) at accounting for variation among marital history categories. Both models were relatively weak in accounting for variation in hours worked, somewhat stronger in accounting for earnings variation, and quite strong in accounting for variation in hourly wage. This pattern of findings supports the argument, suggested in Chapter 4, that variation in hours worked is idiosyncratic, and difficult to explain with any model. (Other studies of labor supply obtain similarly low proportions of explained variance.) On the other hand, the results for hourly wages suggest that the structural model is quite effective at explaining variation in earning power. Economic rewards are easier to explain than labor supply; this suggests that variation in hourly wages is more highly structured than is variation in labor supply.[2]

The structural and individualist approaches differ significantly in their explanations of the relationship between wages and hours. According to the structural approach, wages and hours are codetermined characteristics of jobs, set by employers. Employees' hours worked are subject to the rules of their employers. Employers in advantaged labor market segments tend to offer full-time jobs at relatively high wages; employers in less advantaged labor market segments are more likely to offer part-time or seasonal jobs at lower wages. According to the individualist approach, wages and hours are determined by the market. Women generally work more hours at higher wages (see discussion of income and substitution effects in Chapter 4). In some cases, employees can vary their hours at will. Those who can't vary their hours face a job market in which employers offer jobs with different combinations of wages and hours. Employees apply for jobs that offer the hours they would like to work at a given wage.[3]

The relationship between wages and hours was explicitly included in the model of annual hours presented in Chapter 4. The individualist model clearly accounts for a significant portion of the relationship between wages and hours. However, the structural model is even more effective in accounting for this relationship. These findings provide more support for the structural argument, that employers set both hours and wages, than for the human capital argument, that employees choose their hours of work at a given wage.

The models tested in Chapter 5 also permit a comparison of the effectiveness of the individualist and structural explanations of racial differences in earnings and wages. (There were no significant racial differences in hours worked to be explained.) The individualist and structural models were about equally effective in accounting for the nonwhite disadvantage in annual earnings. The structural model was slightly more effective than the individualist model in accounting for the nonwhite disadvantage in hourly wage. However, the largest portion of the wage gap between nonwhite and white women is explained by differences in education and occupational status. None of the labor market segmentation variables are as effective as these two human capital variables in accounting for racial differences in hourly wage.

In general, the explanatory power of the structural model is significantly stronger than the explanatory power of the individualist model. The structural model is better able to account for variation in hours, earnings, and wages. It is also better able to account for the relationship between hours and wages. However, the structural model is only slightly better at accounting for racial differences in earnings and wages. In summary, while some of the evidence concerning the models' relative strengths is inconclusive, the evidence which does distinguish between the two models favors the structural approach.

What is clear from this analysis is that the combination of the labor market segmentation, human capital, and family role variables performs significantly better than the human capital and family role variables alone. The analyses point especially to the importance of work experience and firm size in determining women's position in the labor market. These findings indicate that individual and structural factors work together to produce labor market outcomes. Although the approach used here to combine the labor market segmentation, human capital, and family role variables is relatively simple, the greater explanatory power of the structural model suggests the potential for further development of models specifying the relationships among these variables.

The findings regarding labor market outcomes suggest several limitations of the structural model. The model employed here assumes that structural factors define a range of outcomes within which individual factors may make a difference. The model assumes that the effects of labor market segmentation and human capital/family role variables are additive. A more complex model, based on a theory of how structural and individual factors interact, would have even greater explanatory power and provide more insight into the nature of labor market processes. One illustration of this approach was provided in Chapter 5, where the interaction of marital history and firm size was considered. Other researchers have begun to develop models of the interaction between individual and structural factors.[4] More theoretical work is required before a sophisticated interactive model can be developed.

A second limitation of the structural model, at least as presented here, is that it fails to provide tests that would rule out different but equally plausible interpretations of the effects of variables. Human capital theorists argue that the effects of job, firm, and industry characteristics in the labor market segmentation model reflect differences in individual workers' ability, productivity, seniority, etc. In other words, individual factors predispose workers toward some jobs, firms, and industries rather than others. Labor market segmentation theorists argue, on the other hand, that variation in human capital among individuals reflects the effects of differential demand on the part of employers. Employers decide who will be given the opportunity to gain work experience, which employees will be encouraged to stay with the firm, what level of education is needed for particular jobs, which employees will receive on-the-job training, etc. While evidence contradicting human capital interpretations of the relationship between firm size and marital history was presented in Chapter 5 (see discussion of Table 5-3), further work in this area is needed.

7.2   WORK–FAMILY LINKAGES OVER THE LIFE COURSE

This study has provided evidence on the nature of linkages between women's work and family roles over the life course. At the most general level, this study has shown that work affects marital history. Married women who have relatively high labor supply and personal income are more likely to divorce than other women. This finding could be interpreted in several ways. Work may cause marital disruption, perhaps by causing work–family conflicts. Or work may enable women in unhappy marriages to divorce, since they will find it easier to support themselves than women who have lower labor supply or earnings. Research by Booth et al. (1984) suggests that to the extent that work affects the probability of divorce, the latter explanation is the most plausible. However, some of the effects of work on the probability of divorce may actually reflect anticipation of economic need after divorce. As indicated in the time series data in Chapter 3, many women increase their labor supply and earnings before divorce. The data presented here do not allow one to determine to what extent work enables women to divorce or to what extent women anticipate divorce by increasing work activity.

Work characteristics also affect the marital history of divorced women. Divorced women who have relatively low labor supply and personal income are more likely to remarry than other divorced women. It is not clear whether weak attachment to the labor force causes remarriage or whether divorced women who expect to remarry invest less time in work than divorced women who do not expect to remarry.

There is also evidence that marital history affects women's work careers. Over the long term, marriage reduces women's labor supply and personal income, while divorce increases both. The effects of remarriage are similar to those of marriage. These effects of marital history on work are consistent with Becker's theory of the family, which suggests that women make trade-offs between work at home and in the labor market (see later discussion).

The study of the relationship between work and marital history also provides evidence about how family responsibilities affect women's work outcomes. Most research that addresses this issue compares married and never-married women.[5] Never-married women experience economic pressure to work and have few family responsibilities. Married women are generally subject to less pressure to work, and have greater family responsibilities, particularly if they have children. As a result of these different constraints, never-married women have continuous work histories, while married women sacrifice their work careers in favor of family roles.

Divorced women are in an intermediate position. They experience the pressure to work that never-married women do, yet they have generally sacrificed their work careers while married, because of family responsibilities. Divorced women who have custody of children are also affected by their current responsibilities for child care, not just past family responsibilities. Most divorced women resolve this role conflict by working to support themselves and their children, and finding alternative providers of child care. In the short term, the higher labor supply of divorced women is similar to that of never-married women, because of economic need, but their low earning power (i.e., hourly wage) is similar to that of married women because of the effects of past family responsibilities on their work careers. In this respect, the findings from this study confirm those of Hudis (1976) and others. However, by considering the long-term effects of divorce, this study suggests that divorced women eventually raise their earning power to a level approaching that of never-married women. Working women who remain divorced apparently overcome the effects of past family responsibilities on their work careers. For these women, divorce produces a significant and lasting change in their relative investments of time in work and family roles.

The effects of divorce on women's work careers depend on a woman's work and family history prior to divorce. Pre-divorce work experience and fertility have a strong effect on women's economic outcomes after divorce. Women who were homemakers and women who had many children find it more difficult to make adjustments to work after divorce. Early decisions about work and family have a significant effect on later work and family outcomes, which in turn differentially position women to cope with the effects of divorce. The life-course aproach taken here focuses on the effects of work and family *history*, rather than the effects of work and family *plans*. While the lifetime labor supply model developed by economists stresses the importance of early plans, the life-course method focuses on the effects of actual behavior. Although early plans may have a strong influence on behavior, women's work careers and family history may not evolve as planned due to a variety of circumstances. In the event of divorce, women's work histories, not their early life plans, are more important determinants of their ability to support themselves.

7.3   THE LONG-TERM CONSEQUENCES OF DIVORCE

This study has considered how changes in marital status over their life course affect women's economic well-being and labor market outcomes. As expected, divorce has negative effects on women's economic well-being. Compared to married women, divorced women have a lower standard of living, and are more likely to be poor and to receive public assistance. However, while most prior research has focused only on estimating the extent of this economic decline, this study has also considered how divorce affects women's economic well-being over the long term.

The sharp drop in women's standard of living at the time of marital disruption does not appear to be as large as Weitzman's (1985) much-cited figure of 73%, based on California data. Estimates presented in Chapter 3, as well as other estimates based on representative national samples, are in the 30–40% range. While women suffer a sharp drop in economic well-being at the time of divorce, most make at least a partial recovery after several years. Several years after divorce, women's standard of living is about 5 to 20% lower than it was during their marriage. Although these results do not suggest that women suffer no economic deprivation after divorce, their initial decline in economic well-being results in increases, first in labor supply, and later in personal income for many divorced women.

Divorce has a strong and immediate impact on women's labor supply. Their labor force participation and hours worked increase sharply after divorce, and remain at high levels. However, the effect of divorce on women's earning power develops only over the long term. This finding accounts for the mixed results of previous studies on the question of whether there is a wage difference between currently divorced and currently married women. Samples containing more long-term divorced women are more likely to indicate such a difference; samples containing more recently divorced women are less likely to find a difference. Previous research ignored the possibility that the effect on earning power of women's adjustments to divorce may become evident only after a number of years. The long-term evaluation used in this study is crucial for identifying the effect of divorce on wages; it also revealed long-term growth in the annual earnings of divorced women. The effects of divorce on labor supply (and earnings, to the extent that they are affected by labor supply) occur more quickly.

As expected, individual-level human capital measures account for a substantial portion of the effects of divorce on women's personal income. The wage advantage, and to some extent, the earnings advantage, of the long-term divorced is due to their greater work experience. The effects of work experience reflect the cumulative impact of the increased labor supply of divorced women. While increased labor supply does not pay off in terms of hourly wage in the short term, it does pay off over a period of several years. In addition, divorced women are less likely than married women to withdraw from the labor force for any period of time. Long and consistent attachment to the labor force is an important explanation for a significant portion of the increased earning power of the long-term divorced.

A surprising finding which emerged from the analyses conducted here is that labor market segmentation variables also account for the long-term effects of divorce on earnings and wages. Divorced and never-married women are more likely to be located in advantaged labor market segments than are married women. A substantial portion of the earnings and wage advantages of divorced women is accounted for by their employment in these advantaged labor market segments. A closer examination of the effects of labor market segmentation indicates that firm size is the key dimension of segmentation in these analyses. Divorced and never-married women are more likely than married women to work in large firms, which pay women significantly more than small firms do.

The findings regarding labor market segmentation and marital history can be interpreted in at least two ways. A weak interpretation is that labor market segmentation on the basis of marital history is due to self-selection on the part of divorced and never-married women. According to this interpretation, divorced and never-married women actively seek employment in large firms, while married women are more likely to accept employment in small firms, which may offer more flexible working hours and be located closer to home. This interpretation assumes that married women have the opportunity to decide whether to work in large or small firms (i.e., that employers in large and in small firms are equally willing to hire them), and that married women themselves choose to work in lower-paying small firms.

A stronger interpretation of the labor market segmentation findings is that there are differences in the demand for women's labor depending on their marital history. If firms prefer to hire single women rather than married women, one would expect to find, as the analyses show, that a disproportionately large number of divorced and never-married women work in large firms. This disproportionate representation of single women in large firms would be expected even if all women, regardless of marital history, prefer to work in high-paying (i.e., large) firms. Large firms can pay more to attract the type of employees that they want. Small firms generally lose out in this competition because they cannot pay high enough salaries to attract and keep the most desirable types of employees. Large firms have longer promotion ladders and offer a wider range of salaries than smaller firms, which have fewer promotion opportunities and cannot afford to pay relatively high salaries. In this view, the labor market advantage of single women is due to employers' decisions, independent of the preferences and choices of married and divorced women.

Additional evidence that large firms prefer divorced and never-married women is provided in the analysis of wage differentials by marital history within firm size categories. Within large firms, long-term divorced and never-married women earn higher wages than married women, even after controlling for differences in human capital. The preference for single women is indicated not only by the fact that large firms are more likely to hire single women, but also by the fact that they pay single women more than married women, even after controlling for human capital differences between single and married women. Within small firms, marital history differences are not significant.

While it is impossible using the data available here to decide whether the strong (employer-demand) or weak (self-selection) interpretation of labor market segmentation differences is more accurate, the evidence on wage differentials within large firms favors the strong interpretation. There is certainly sufficient evidence to re-open the question of whether employers prefer single women over married women. As reviewed in Chapter 1, most studies have concluded that an employer preference for single women over married women ended by 1960. Data here suggest that such a preference continued at least into the late 1970s.

Since employers often justify gender inequality by arguing that women are less reliable and productive than men because of their obligations to their husbands and children, it is not surprising that employers might believe that single women are better employees than married women. The double bind for women, of course, has always been that employers expect that single women will marry and have children. "Singleness" may be used by employers as a sign of stability, reliability, and commitment to work only for older women who have remained single (such as the never-married and long-term divorced women considered here), and whom employers may expect will not (re)marry. Employers may not believe that "singleness" is a useful sign of stability, reliability, and commitment to work for young women, since employers may expect that most young single women will marry. The importance of remaining single over a long period of time is indicated by the finding that the preference for single women in large firms includes long-term divorced but not recently divorced women. Employers may believe that long-term divorced women are not likely to remarry, while they may be less certain about whether recently divorced women will do so.

This interpretation of the labor market segmentation findings suggests that employers discriminate among women by marital history for one of the same reasons they discriminate against women in favor of men. They believe that marriage and children interfere with women's employment. Siebert and Sloane argue that "employers might unjustifiably regard marital status as a proxy for commitment to work, indicating employment instability in the case of married women but stability in the case of married men."[6] The fact that older never-married women do not fare as well as men suggests that employers also discriminate against women for other reasons. Employers may believe that women as a group are generally less productive employees than men.

Results from the explanatory models suggest that divorce affects the behavior of both employees and employers. It could be argued that these behavioral changes are interdependent, i.e. that employers' preferences for divorced women are a response to changes in work behavior by divorced women, and/or that divorced women's movement into advantaged labor market segments is a response to changes in the behavior of employers (i.e., their greater willingness to hire and reward single women). This argument is partially supported, insofar as there is considerable overlap in the explanatory power of the individualist and structural models. However, it is also clear that the structural model provides a more complete explanation of the marital history differences than does the individualist model, suggesting that structural factors have an independent effect. Even after controlling for individual factors, segmentation variables (primarily firm size) account for an additional portion of the labor market advantage for divorced women. As noted above, what is most surprising about these results is the finding that women who have different marital histories are not randomly distributed among labor market segments. If the strong interpretation offered above is correct, then the labor market disadvantage of married women relative to divorced and never-married women is at least partly the result of discrimination against married women, and not solely (or even primarily) the result of trade-offs women make between time spent at work and in family roles.

The earnings and wage advantages of divorced women that remain unexplained in the structural model point to the need for the development of new measures of labor market segmentation, human capital, and family role variables. Clearly, the standard measures of human capital and of labor market segmentation do not capture some of the more subtle aspects of the effects of divorce. Data on work commitment might indicate that divorced women are more willing than married women to make sacrifices for higher-paying jobs. For example, Moen and Smith (1986) found that unmarried women had a stronger commitment to work than married women; unfortunately, they did not differentiate among divorced, separated, and never-married women. On the other hand, measures of employers' attitudes regarding work commitment, reliability, or productivity of married and divorced women might indicate that employers believe divorced women are better employees.

A more complete understanding of the adjustments that accompany marital disruption requires detailed consideration of changes occurring just prior to, and immediately after, divorce. These changes are critical for understanding the long-term consequences of divorce identified here.[7] Data on mobility among labor market segments would help to interpret the structural effects. If married women in advantaged labor market segments are more likely to divorce than those in less advantaged segments, then job pressures or opportunities for advancement in advantaged segments may increase the likelihood of divorce. However, evidence indicating that mobility into advantaged segments after divorce is common would provide support for either the employer-demand or self-selection explanations discussed above. Felmlee's (1984) study of women's job mobility indicates that married women are less likely than unmarried women to shift from one full-time job to another. Since such shifts are associated with wage increases, this finding may account, at least in part, for the higher wages of unmarried women. Felmlee argues that married women don't have the flexibility to make transitions from one full-time job to another (the self-selection argument). It may also be that employers are more willing to hire unmarried women (the employer-demand argument). More research is needed regarding how the behavior of employers and employees changes in response to a woman's divorce. It would also be interesting to consider whether divorce has a contrasting negative effect on men's careers, since divorce is generally seen as a sign of instability in men, while married men who have children are regarded as stable workers.

This study has also considered how variation among women with respect to work and family history affects economic well-being after divorce. The analysis of economic well-being, designed to focus on the impact of prior life history on post-divorce outcomes, was confined to the effects of individual characteristics and ignored structural features of the labor market. As expected, work experience before divorce was found to be an important determinant of economic well-being after divorce. In particular, women who were homemakers during marriage experience especially severe economic problems after divorce. These women have a more difficult time gaining work experience after divorce and are more likely to have children in the household than other divorced women. These findings are consistent with Weitzman's argument that homemakers in marriages of long duration and women who have children are among those most negatively affected by divorce. However, while Weitzman argues that women who were intermittent workers have as much difficulty earning a living as homemakers do after divorce,[8] data from this study indicate that intermittent workers are more similar to women who worked continuously than they are to homemakers. This discrepancy in findings may be due to differences between a short-term and a long-term evaluation. Intermittent workers may experience economic hardship in the year immediately after divorce (the time period Weitzman considered). However, after several years of adjustment and job search, these women may be able to capitalize on past experience and improve their economic situation.

While a middle-class woman may feel protected from economic hardship, her spouse's middle-class income does not guarantee her economic security in the event of divorce. As Weitzman has shown, courts rarely require husbands to support their ex-wives on an adequate income for any length of time. Data from this study show that alimony and child support payments, while they are targeted toward some of the neediest divorced women, are nevertheless insufficient to significantly reduce the number of divorced women who are poor and/or receiving public assistance. However, while Weitzman argues that most divorced women end up in the "underclass" or "second tier" of society, data from this study indicate that a significant minority do not. Over 35% of the divorced women in this study had an above-average standard of living[9] (compared with 60% of continuously married women). While married women have a higher standard of living, on average, than divorced women, there is, nevertheless, significant variation among divorced women.

This study, unlike Weitzman's, has focused on work history, rather than social class, to examine variation in women's economic well-being after divorce. This approach recognizes that marriage to a spouse with a middle-class income does not provide a woman with economic security in the event of divorce. In addition, it recognizes that there is significant variation in economic well-being among divorced women. Work history accounts for a significant portion of this variation. Work during marriage provides greater economic security for a woman than does marriage to a middle-income spouse.

Separation, unlike divorce, has few positive effects on labor market behavior. While the economic problems of divorced women are often cited as a major cause of the "feminization of poverty," many poor women are separated but not divorced. The economic problems of separated women, as documented here, are worse than those of divorced women. Separation is, for some women, a temporary stage before divorce. For women making this transition, separation may be a period of severe economic difficulty. Recently separated women who are re-entering the labor market, or who are seeking to make their employment full-time, may experience difficulties in finding a job, satisfactory living arrangements, and child care. While the situation of these recently separated women may improve after divorce, most women identified as separated in this study had been separated for at least several years, and did not appear to be making the transition to divorce. In some cases, these long-term separated women were too poor to afford a divorce; many received public assistance. On almost every measure of work and family characteristics, separated women are at a greater disadvantage than divorced women. They are more likely to have children, they have fewer years of education and work experience, and they are employed in the least desirable jobs. Separated women, rather than divorced women, represent the more disadvantaged of these "female-headed households," and should be more often addressed in discussions of public policy.

A very large proportion of the long-term separated women are nonwhite. Their poverty, inadequate job training, unsteady work, and undesirable jobs may all be results of racism. Economic differences between separated and divorced women may therefore reflect the effects of racial differences between the two groups rather than differences between the effects of separation and of divorce.

Since there is some overlap between the questions addressed in this book and those addressed in Weitzman's *The Divorce Revolution*, this section concludes with a comparison of the two studies. While they are both concerned with the economic consequences of divorce for women, there are important differences in emphasis between the two studies.

First, Weitzman compares the economic well-being of divorced women to their former spouses'. As a result, the gap she finds between the standards of living of divorced husbands and wives is due in large part to gender inequality in the labor market, not necessarily to gender inequity in divorce laws. The analyses presented here compare divorced women to married women, who provide a more appropriate benchmark against which to judge the outcomes of divorced women. The economic outcomes of married women represent the best estimate of the expected outcomes of divorced women, had they not divorced.

Second, both studies find a decline in economic well-being after divorce, but Weitzman's estimates of that decline are larger than those in this study. Furthermore, this study finds that, over time, divorced women improve their standard of living; Weitzman focuses only on the immediate, short-term decline.[10]

Third, this book does not evaluate the legal aspects of the divorce process. It is not concerned with the laws governing distribution of assets or child custody, and only indirectly concerned with those governing alimony and child support. Undoubtedly, Weitzman's recommendations regarding divorce law would improve the economic situation of significant numbers of divorced women, particularly middle-class women. Changes in divorce law would not help poor women as much, since many do not obtain a legal divorce, and those who do are unlikely to obtain adequate support payments, since their spouses' incomes are low. Furthermore, since young women are increasingly planning to spend most of their adult years in the labor market, it is not clear that reforms that recognize the contribution of traditional homemakers will help many young women in the future. A decline in gender inequality in the labor market would do more to reduce the gap in standards of living between divorced women and men.

7.4 CHANGING GENDER ROLES—A GENERATION IN TRANSITION

The cohort of women considered in this book came of age at a time when women were expected to give priority to family over work roles. However, through the 1960s and 1970s social expectations began to change and, for a variety of reasons, women entered (or re-entered) the labor force in larger numbers, and gave greater priority to work roles. This transition in women's roles caught many women in this cohort unprepared, especially those who experienced a marital disruption. Women who had expected to give priority to caring for their families found that they were expected to be ready to earn enough to support themselves and their children.

There is considerable evidence that this generation of women made trade-offs between work and marriage. Married women worked less than never-married women. When women experienced economic need as a result of divorce, they worked more; when they remarried, they worked less. Most women of this cohort had apparently established a stable preference for household work over work in the labor market. They apparently emphasized paid work activities only out of necessity (e.g., in response to marital disruption).

While the *patterns* of findings regarding work and marital history are consistent with the human capital argument that women trade off between paid work and household work, the *explanation* of these patterns may not be. For example, as was pointed out in Chapter 3, it is difficult to sort out the relative importance of economic need or taste for work as factors encouraging women to work. If divorced women work more hours not because of economic need but because, even while married, they were women who had a greater taste for work, the human capital argument concerning trade-offs is not supported. Some evidence presented in Chapter 3 would appear to be consistent with the argument that divorced women had a greater taste for work. Married women who were about to become divorced were more likely than other married women to work, to work longer hours, and to have higher earnings and wages. Yet this evidence can also be interpreted to suggest that economic need, and not taste for work, was the major factor inducing changes in work behavior of divorced women. The stronger labor force attachment of married women who became divorced might reflect anticipation of economic need and not taste for work. Furthermore, the models of labor supply indicate that human capital variables and egalitarian gender attitudes (which should reflect taste for work) do not account for differences in labor supply between recently divorced and continuously married women.

In summary, while the effects of economic need and taste for work are difficult to untangle, the explanatory models lend more credence to the "economic need" interpretation. In this respect, then, the explanation of these results supports the assumption that women trade off between household work and work in the labor market.

Other findings from this study, however, contradict this assumption. The evidence regarding structural effects suggests that part of the explanation for the greater earnings capacity of never-married and divorced women is greater employer demand for these women as employees. Married women may emphasize household work over work in the labor market not solely because of individual preference, but also because employer demand for their labor is weak relative to the demand for labor of men and single women. Employers apparently act on their expectation that household responsibilities interfere with work activity. The pattern of apparent trade-offs observed here can also be explained as the result of structural constraints in the labor market.

Evidence presented in Chapter 6 regarding changes in life plans by divorced women also contradicts Becker's (1981) assumption concerning women's trade-offs. Some women who remained divorced for a long period of time became more work-oriented, did not remarry, and followed labor market patterns similar to those of never-married women. In response to an unexpected life event, these women, whether by choice or necessity, changed their preferences regarding household and market labor. While Becker argues that women have a stable preference for household over market labor, many long-term divorced women have established new preferences, by giving priority to work in the labor market and by not remarrying. This category is small relative to the number of women who have maintained a stable preference over the life cycle. It is nevertheless theoretically important because it illustrates how a life event can alter a seemingly stable preference.

Finally, evidence on labor market outcomes of divorced women who have children calls into question the ability of Becker's model to make predictions about trade-offs between work at home and work in the labor market. The wage advantage of divorced women over married women is slightly *stronger* among those who have children than among those who do not have children. As noted in Chapter 5, this finding can be viewed as consistent with human capital theory if children are viewed as providing an economic incentive to work, or as inconsistent with the theory if children are viewed as a burden inhibiting work effort. Since the theory views children in both ways (although more often as a burden), it provides little guidance either for generating hypotheses about work behavior of divorced women who have children, or for interpreting these findings.

This failure to provide a clear prediction is symptomatic of the theory's failure to deal adequately with the complexity of choices and especially the particular constraints that women face. In addition to trading off between their own work and reliance on their spouses' income, women trade off between providing financial support for their children and investing time in caring for their children. Investing time in work and in child care are thus alternative ways of giving priority to children. Divorced women invest time at work to provide financial support for their children, while married women spend more time in child care.

This trade-off can be interpreted in different ways. One could argue that women prefer to spend time in child care and work only out of necessity (i.e., if they become divorced). Or one could argue that married women are constrained to invest their time in child care, and that when freed from this constraint, they prefer to work. It is also possible that many women are committed to both work *and* family, but curtail their work activity because of family constraints.[11] Among the constraints pushing married women to invest time in child care are low-paying jobs, blocked mobility at work, lack of affordable day care, their husbands' traditional expectations, and their husbands' lack of involvement in child care (see Gerson 1985 for a full discussion of these factors). Furthermore, many women change their work and family commitments in response to constraints and opportunities. While women in this cohort apparently made trade-offs between work and family, these trade-offs do not necessarily reflect individual preferences. Trade-offs can also represent a balancing of constraints, such as balancing the need for family income against the need for child care. Both married and divorced women may feel they are balancing conflicting demands. The interplay of both structural factors and individual preferences affects the trade-offs women make between work and family.

This study has indicated the importance of work for the economic well-being of divorced women and their children. Married women who give priority to child care rather than to paid work (whether through personal preference or because of constraints) are at a significant disadvantage in the event of divorce. Homemakers have a lower standard of living, and are more likely to be poor and to receive public assistance than other women after divorce. While post-divorce work adjustments can improve the standard of living of divorced women, making these adjustments is harder for homemakers than for other women. Women who worked at least intermittently fare better than homemakers after divorce, and find it easier to make work adjustments. Surprisingly, women who worked continuously did not fare better than those who worked intermittently. Apparently women who worked intermittently were able to capitalize on their experience to obtain jobs as well-paying as those of women who worked continuously. This finding suggests that women who were continuous workers were not employed in jobs with significant rewards for seniority, whether because of their own choices or because of discrimination in the labor market. As a result, even these women were not well-prepared to support themselves.

This cohort of women, which early in life faced opportunities and constraints promoting investment of their time in marriage and children rather than paid work, faced a different set of expectations in middle age. These women, even those who worked continuously, made career sacrifices in favor of their family commitments. Yet, as Weitzman (1985) notes, when these women experienced divorce, judges did not compensate them for having made these sacrifices.

Younger women, on the other hand, experience more incentives to work and have more opportunities in the work place. It is increasingly the case that both of the spouses must work for a family to maintain a middle-class standard of living. The message for younger women is clear. They are expected to work and to be able to support themselves in the event of divorce. As others have noted, this expectation requires women to balance both work and child care, and places unrealistic demands on women's time. Yet, it is clear that work gives women greater long-term economic security than does marriage. This was the case for the older cohort of women considered in this study; work is even more important as a source of economic security for young women today.

APPENDIX A

Description of Variables Employed in the Analysis

Data on the distributions of variables discussed in this Appendix are presented in Appendix B. Appendix C presents the distributions within each marital history group.

A.1 DEPENDENT VARIABLES

Labor Supply. As Killingsworth (1983, pp. 97–98) notes, there are several conceptual dimensions of labor supply and many empirical measures available for each dimension. The four conceptual dimensions are: total labor supply, the structural labor supply schedule, labor force participation, and the labor supply of workers (Killingsworth 1983, p. 180). This study focuses on the latter two aspects of labor supply. In most cases, labor force participation is measured as a dichotomous variable using the standard U.S. Bureau of the Census definition—coded "0" for those not working and not actively seeking work, coded "1" for those working or actively seeking work in the week prior to the interview. However, in the explanatory model of labor force participation (Table 4-1), workers are defined as those who worked any hours in the previous year (see the discussion in Chapter 4, Section 2). Three measures of the labor supply of workers are available in the National Longitudinal Surveys of Mature Women (NLS): usual hours worked per week, weeks worked per year, and the product of these two, annual hours worked. The last measure has been chosen here because it reflects the effects of part-time and of part-year work. Dual labor market theorists argue that annual hours are a characteristic of the job a person holds and reflect demand for labor, not supply (Beck et al. 1980). Workers may, however, seek jobs that offer their desired hours of work (Killingsworth 1983, p. 18). Appelbaum (1981) demonstrates that many women work part-time voluntarily, and that lack of adequate child care may affect willingness to work full-time and/or year-round. Annual hours may reflect both demand for *and* supply of labor. Both types of models are developed in Chapter 4.

Wage. The wage reported in this study, unless otherwise indicated, is hourly wage at current job. Wages were computed from the response to the question: "Altogether, how much do you usually earn at this job before deductions?"; wage was *not* computed by dividing total annual earnings by annual hours worked. Where data on wages are presented for years other than 1977 (e.g., time series data in Chapter 3), figures are adjusted to 1977 dollars based on the consumer price index (CPI).

Earnings. Earnings consist of all income received from wages, salary, commissions, and tips, before deductions, in the year preceding the interview. Where earnings data are presented for years other than 1976, figures are adjusted to 1976 dollars, based on the CPI.

Family Income. While total family income in the year prior to each survey is already computed on the NLS data tape, this computed variable is not used, for two reasons. First, there was too much missing data, since total income was coded "missing" if any one of up to 30 components of income was missing. Second, the NLS measure included the value of food stamps, which was not considered by the Census Bureau as cash income in the years the study was conducted. To compute family income for the present study, the components of income, excluding food stamps, are summed. Where data on earnings for the woman and/or her spouse (if present and working) and/or other family members (if present and working) are missing, then family income is coded "missing." When data are missing for other categories of income, the amount of income in that category is assumed to be zero. This assumption results in only a slight downward bias in the measurement of income for families with missing data. The expected value in those other categories is close to zero, since the proportion of families who have income in any one of those other categories is low, and the mean for those who have income in any one of those categories is also low. Cases where the respondent refused to answer one or more of the earnings questions or where answers to over one-third of the income questions are missing for other reasons (e.g., "don't know" or interviewer forgot to record) are coded "missing" for family income. Where family income data are presented for years other than 1976, figures are adjusted to 1976 dollars, based on the CPI.

Income/Needs Ratio. The income/needs ratio is computed by dividing total family income by the poverty threshold. The poverty threshold varies depending on family size (see discussion of poverty status which follows).

Poverty Status. The measure of poverty status used here is based on the U.S. Census definition, but takes into consideration only the Census adjustment for family size. Information on farm versus nonfarm residence is not available in the NLS, and no adjustments for heads of households over 65 are made (very few households in the survey were in this category, given that the women were aged 30 through 44 in 1967). The Census assumption that households with female heads can live on less money than households with male heads is viewed as untenable, so no adjustments for sex of head are made. A family is considered to be poor if its family income is below the poverty threshold for its family size.

Public Assistance Status. Respondents who reported receiving income from

Supplemental Security Income (SSI), Aid to Families with Dependent Children (AFDC), or other public assistance programs are coded as receiving public assistance.

A.2 RACE

Nonwhite. Cases are coded "0' if their race was recorded as "white," and "1" if their race was recorded as "black" or "other." Since there were only 87 cases coded "other," and since blacks were oversampled (see discussion in Chapter 2), the vast majority of those classified as nonwhite are black.

A.3 LABOR MARKET SEGMENTATION VARIABLES

Labor Market Sector. Labor market sector is operationalized according to the classification system used in Tolbert et al. (1980). Individuals are classified as working in the core or periphery sectors depending on the industry in which they work. Since Tolbert et al. (1980) used the 1970 Standard Industrial Classifications to determine sector, the 1960 classification available in the NLS was converted to the 1970 classification, based on data available in Priebe et al. (1972).

Firm Size. Firm size was asked only in 1977, and coded in 6 categories. To transform this variable to a roughly interval measure, each category is coded as the midpoint of the logarithm of its endpoints. The largest category (1,000 or more employees) is coded as the logarithm of 1,200, since no maximum value is available as an endpoint.

Union Status. Union status is a dummy variable coded "1" if the respondent was a member of a union at her place of employment, "0" otherwise.

Other Job Characteristics. Job characteristics include decision latitude, supervisory status, and job insecurity. While none of these dimensions was measured directly in the NLS, scores for each job characteristic are imputed for each case based on a procedure developed by Schwartz (Karasek et al. 1983a) using the Quality of Employment Survey (QES). The decision latitude scale includes items such as skill level, variety of work, opportunity to develop new skills, ability to make decisions, and freedom in determining how to perform work. Supervisory status is a measure of the probability of a worker being a supervisor, given her occupation and demographic characteristics. The job insecurity measure includes QES respondents' ratings of their job insecurity, the steadiness of their jobs, and their likelihood of being laid off. Evidence on the validity and reliability of these measures for women is provided in Karasek et al. (1983b). A discussion of the power of the technique of imputing scores to data sets other than the QES is included in Schwartz and Pieper (1982).

For each job characteristic a mean scale score for each 3-digit Census occupation was calculated using data from the QES surveys of 1969, 1972, and 1977. Equations were then developed to adjust the means for certain demographic characteristics, thereby predicting some variation within occupations, improving the efficiency of estimates, and reducing bias. These adjusted means for each occupation were imputed to the NLS data, and modified using the equations developed in the QES. This procedure is similar to that used to link QES data to the Health and Nutrition Examination Survey (Karasek et al. 1983a).

A.4   HUMAN CAPITAL VARIABLES

Education. Education is measured as years of schooling completed. No attempt is made to measure quality of education. (While a measure of school quality is available for the two younger cohorts in the NLS, no such measure is available for the NLS cohort considered here.) Models were tested which included dummy variables for the effect of educational credentials (i.e., degrees received), and measures of years of education beyond high school and beyond college. Including these variables only marginally improved the explanatory power of human capital models, and did not affect conclusions regarding the effects of marital history. For these reasons, years of schooling completed is the only measure of education used in this study.

Work Experience. Work experience is measured using two variables: total years of work experience since completing school and total years working for current employer. While a question concerning years with current employer was asked directly, the measure of total years of work experience is more problematic:

> The measure of general labor market experience prior to the initial survey for the cohort of mature women has some undesirable properties. Respondents reported the *number of years in which they worked at least six months*. If total weeks of experience is the appropriate indicator, then the NLS item will tend to have errors that are positively correlated with true experience. For example, women who consistently work between 27 and 51 weeks will have their experience overstated (since they will be attributed a full year of experience), while those who consistently work between 1 and 25 weeks per year will have theirs understated (since they will be attributed zero weeks of experience). (Hawley and Bielby 1978, p. 89, emphasis added)

The measure of total years of work experience is really a measure of total years in which the respondent worked six months or more. While this measure may not be quite as accurate as one could wish, it is more precise than measures often used in national surveys (see, for example, Corcoran's (1979a) discussion of the work experience measure in the Panel Study of Income Dynamics).

Since the work experience measure for 1967 was defined as the number of years in which the respondent worked six months or more, the same definition was used to update the work experience measure to 1977. Unfortunately, data on weeks worked were not available for 1972 and 1974, so the measure of total years of experience in 1977 assumes there were only eight (rather than ten) years of potential experience between 1967 and 1977.

Years at current job, a second measure of work experience, is also available for working women. It is used in addition to the total work experience measure to pick up the effects of firm-specific training, the importance of which is suggested by human capital theory.

A measure of potential work experience, years since school, is used in the models of labor force participation in Chapter 4 and in Appendix D. Years since school is computed as age minus education minus 6.

Received Occupational Training. This measure is coded as a dummy variable: "1" if the woman has taken a training course since leaving school, "0" otherwise.

Occupational Status. Occupational status is measured using Bose scores of occupational prestige, which are more appropriate than Duncan scores when data for women are analyzed. Bose (1973) computed occupational status scores by updating Duncan's Socioeconomic Index (SEI) regression equation (Blau and Duncan 1967) to 1960, using weights derived from data on women's rather than men's income and education.

A.5   FAMILY ROLE VARIABLES

Characteristics of Other Adult Family Members. Characteristics of other adult family members include their earnings and hours worked. Each is represented both by a dummy variable (whether any other family member had earnings or had worked any hours in the previous year) and by the sum of earnings and the sum of hours worked by all other family members. If there are no other adult family members, all these variables are coded "0."

Children. The effects of children are measured by several variables: whether a woman has children in the household, the number of children in the household, and whether a woman has children under 5 years old in the household. Since by 1977 many of the children had grown up and left the household, and few of the women still had young children, an additional measure, total fertility, is also used. Total fertility is the number of children a woman has had, regardless of whether or not they currently live in her household.

Egalitarian Gender Attitudes. The scale of egalitarian gender attitudes was developed in the following manner: Nine items (with responses ranging from 1 to 5, "strongly agree" to "strongly disagree") that measure attitudes toward women's work and family roles were factor-analyzed using principal components. Results from a one-factor solution indicated that 4 of the items loaded more highly on the scale than the other 5. A two-factor solution confirmed the presence of two factors. However, the second factor appeared to be a method artifact (Carmines and Zeller 1979), since the 5 items were all worded in an "egalitarian" direction, while the 4 questions in the first factor were all worded in a "traditional" direction. To determine whether this second factor was a method artifact, a two-factor solution was derived using LISREL, where the second factor was orthogonal and fixed, with "egalitarian" items coded − 1 and "traditional" items coded + 1. The LISREL model explained only 33% of the variance in the items, compared with 48% explained by the two-factor solution using principal components. These results suggest that the second factor is not a method artifact, but a scale measuring some other attitudinal dimension.

Further support for this conclusion was provided through a check for construct validity. Two scales were constructed (by summing items, since factor score coefficients were about equal for the items on each factor). The scales are only moderately correlated with each other (r = .39). The scale corresponding to the first factor is related to other variables in expected ways (for example, women who have egalitarian attitudes have fewer children and more years of education), while the scale corresponding to the second factor is only weakly related to these same variables (indeed, sometimes the correlation has the "wrong" sign). Because of the weak construct validity of the second factor and the likelihood that it is not a method artifact, the scale of egalitarian gender attitudes was developed using only items that loaded on the first factor. These items were scored in such a way that a high score indicated an egalitarian response. Cronbach's alpha for this scale is .78, a reasonably high reliability. This measure of gender attitudes is available only for 1977, since these items were not asked in 1967. Details on the items in this scale are provided in Table A-1.

A.6   WORK ORIENTATION MEASURE

Pre-divorce work orientation is measured using dummy variables, and is based

TABLE A–1:
Items Analyzed for Egalitarian Gender Attitudes Scale

Question: "We are interested in your opinion about the employment of wives. I will read you a series of statements and after each one I would like to know whether you: strongly agree, agree, disagree, or strongly disagree?"

Items included in the scale	Mean[a]	Standard Deviation
"A woman's place is in the home, not in the office or shop."	3.32	1.14
"A wife who carries out her full family responsibilities doesn't have time for outside employment."	3.30	1.12
"The employment of wives leads to more juvenile delinquency."	3.01	1.17
"Working wives lose interest in their homes and families."	3.72	1.01
Items not included in the scale		
"Modern conveniences permit a wife to work without neglecting her family."	3.48	1.06
"A job provides a wife with interesting outside contacts."	3.89	0.76

[a] Items were scored so that a high score indicates an egalitarian response, i.e., items included in the scale were coded: strongly agree = 1, agree = 2, undecided = 3, disagree = 4, strongly disagree = 5, while items not included in the scale were coded: strongly agree = 5, agree = 4, undecided = 3, disagree = 2, and strongly disagree = 1. Data presented are for the 3,854 cases with complete data for all the items.

TABLE A–1—*Continued*

Items included in the scale	Mean[a]	Standard Deviation
"A working wife feels more useful than one who doesn't hold a job."	3.24	1.11
"Working wives help to raise the general standard of living."	3.91	0.73
"Employment of both parents is necessary to keep up with the high cost of living."	3.77	1.04

on the percentage of years worked between leaving school and the time of divorce. Women who worked less than 20% of those years are coded "1" on a homemaker dummy variable, "0" otherwise. Women who worked more than 80% of those years are coded "1" on a career dummy variable, "0" otherwise. The remaining category is intermittent workers, a category that includes women who worked between 20% and 80% of those years.

APPENDIX B

Descriptive Statistics for Variables Employed in the Analysis

TABLE B–1:
Descriptive Statistics for Interval Variables

Variables	Mean	Standard Deviation	Skewness[a]	(Number)
Dependent Variables				
Hours, 1966	1,440.00	810.00	−0.06	(2,162)
Hours, 1966 (Ln)	6.96	1.02	−1.80	(2,162)
Hours, 1976	1,613.00	700.00	−0.36	(2,307)
Hours, 1976 (Ln)	7.20	0.79	−2.45	(2,307)
Wage, 1967	1.90	1.00	2.26	(1,716)
Wage, 1967 (Ln)	0.51	0.54	−0.61	(1,716)
Wage, 1977	4.05	2.17	3.91	(1,979)
Wage, 1977 (Ln)	1.29	0.47	−0.08	(1,979)
Earnings, 1966	2,670.00	2,250.00	1.07	(2,109)
Earnings, 1966 (Ln)	7.34	1.28	−1.09	(2,109)
Earnings, 1976	6,420.00	5,230.00	2.24	(2,179)
Earnings, 1976 (Ln)	8.36	1.11	−1.41	(2,179)
Family income, 1966	7,680.00	5,490.00	1.96	(3,909)
Family income, 1966 (Ln)	8.40	1.82	−3.49	(3,909)
Family income, 1976	15,740.00	12,450.00	1.36	(3,671)
Family income, 1976 (Ln)	8.87	2.32	−2.97	(3,671)
Income/needs ratio, 1966	2.31	1.70	2.01	(3,776)
Income/needs ratio, 1966 (Ln)	0.50	1.00	−2.21	(3,776)
Income/needs ratio, 1976	3.25	2.45	1.75	(3,474)
Income/needs ratio, 1976 (Ln)	0.82	1.05	−2.00	(3,474)
Labor Market Segmentation Variables				
Decision latitude, 1977	4.24	0.15		(2,275)
Job insecurity, 1977	1.58	0.17		(2,315)
Supervisory status, 1977	0.30	0.20		(2,323)

(Continued on next page)

TABLE B-1—*Continued*

Variables	Mean	Standard Deviation	Skewness[a]	(Number)
Firm size, 1977	405.00	494.00	0.81	(2,207)
Firm size, 1977 (Ln)	4.44	2.22	−0.17	(2,207)
Human Capital Variables				
Education, 1977	11.45	2.84		(3,887)
Years since school, 1977	30.94	5.54		(3,950)
Years of work experience, 1977	13.94	8.79		(3,330)
Years at current job, 1977	6.57	6.50		(2,006)
Occupational status, 1977 (Bose)	44.88	16.65		(2,240)
Family Role Variables				
Earnings, other household members, 1976	9,060.00	10,450.00	1.23	(3,752)
Earnings, other household members, 1976 (Ln)	5.92	4.45	−0.50	(3,752)
Hours worked by other household members, 1976	2,100.00	1,720.00		(3,962)
Egalitarian gender attitudes, 1977	13.34	3.44		(3,876)
Number of children in household, 1977	1.08	1.43		(3,964)
Number of children in household under age five, 1977	0.02	0.18		(3,964)
Total fertility, 1977	3.39	2.52		(3,964)
Age, 1977	47.92	4.41		(3,964)

Ln = Natural logarithm transformation.
[a] Reported only for variables transformed for analysis.

TABLE B-2: *Descriptive Statistics for Dichotomous Variables*

Variables	Percentage of Cases in Category	(Number)
Dependent Variables		
In the labor force, 1977	60%	(3,964)
Poor, 1976	20%	(3,671)
Received public assistance, 1976	10%	(3,941)

(Continued on next page)

TABLE B–2—*Continued*

Variables	Percentage of Cases in Category	(Number)
Race		
Nonwhite	28%	(3,960)
Labor Market Segmentation Variables		
Union membership, 1977	16%	(2,397)
Core industry, 1977	34%	(2,381)
Human Capital Variable		
Received occupational training, 1977	49%	(3,212)
Family Role Variables		
Any other earners in household, 1976	65%	(3,752)
Any children in household, 1977	51%	(3,964)
Any children in household under age five, 1977	2%	(3,964)

TABLE B–3: *Distribution of Work Orientation, 1967*

Work Orientation	Percentage Distribution
Homemaker	27%
Intermittent worker	52
Career woman	21
Total	100%
(Number)	(3,436)

Descriptive Statistics for Variables by Marital History

TABLE C–1: *Income/Needs Ratio*[a]

		Year				
		1966			1976	
Marital History	Mean	Standard Deviation	(Number)	Mean	Standard Deviation	(Number)
Married throughout	2.55	1.74	(2,153)	3.75	2.50	(1,988)
Recently divorced	2.46	2.09	(168)	2.36	1.59	(157)
Long-term divorced	1.61	1.18	(165)	2.46	2.10	(154)
Never married	2.11	1.63	(155)	2.64	2.44	(144)
Recently separated	1.84	1.32	(94)	1.67	2.20	(82)
Long-term separated	0.85	0.63	(83)	1.20	1.05	(70)
Remarried throughout	2.53	1.72	(256)	3.49	2.54	(244)
Remarried, divorced after 1967	2.38	1.62	(75)	3.74	2.67	(70)
Remarried, divorced in 1967	1.58	1.12	(74)	3.30	2.69	(65)
Other	1.86	1.53	(553)	2.35	1.91	(500)
Total, all cases	2.31	1.70	(3,776)	3.25	2.45	(3,474)

[a] Distributions of other dependent variables within each marital history group are presented in Chapter 3.

TABLE C–2: *Proportion Nonwhite*

	Estimate				
	Unweighted		Weighted		
Marital history	Mean	Standard Deviation	Mean	Standard Deviation	(Number)
Married throughout	.18	.39	.07	.27	(2,273)
Recently divorced	.28	.45	.12	.33	(172)
Long-term divorced	.45	.50	.22	.39	(170)
Never married	.38	.49	.14	.33	(164)
Recently separated	.59	.49	.33	.41	(101)
Long-term separated	.93	.26	.84	.23	(84)
Remarried throughout	.28	.45	.10	.31	(267)
Remarried, divorced after 1967	.20	.40	.07	.25	(81)
Remarried, divorced in 1967	.34	.48	.13	.33	(76)
Other	.47	.50	.22	.38	(572)
Total, all cases	.28	.45	.12	.32	(3,960)

TABLE C–3: *Labor Market Segmentation Variables*

a. DECISION LATITUDE, CURRENT JOB

	Year					
	1967			1977		
Marital History	Mean	Standard Deviation	(Number)	Mean	Standard Deviation	(Number)
Married throughout	4.24	.16	(981)	4.26	.15	(1,232)
Recently divorced	4.22	.14	(89)	4.24	.15	(132)
Long-term divorced	4.18	.15	(135)	4.20	.15	(124)
Never married	4.26	.16	(115)	4.27	.14	(108)
Recently separated	4.18	.14	(52)	4.18	.14	(55)
Long-term separated	4.16	.12	(60)	4.15	.12	(51)
Remarried throughout	4.20	.14	(147)	4.22	.17	(147)
Remarried, divorced after 1967	4.21	.21	(42)	4.26	.18	(52)
Remarried, divorced in 1967	4.20	.14	(60)	4.22	.14	(40)
Other	4.20	.15	(337)	4.21	.16	(334)
Total, all cases	4.22	.16	(2,018)	4.24	.15	(2,275)

(Continued on next page)

TABLE C–3—*Continued*

b. UNION MEMBERSHIP, CURRENT JOB (dichotomous)

Marital History	Mean	Standard Deviation	(Number)
		Year 1977	
Married throughout	.15	.35	(1,301)
Recently divorced	.16	.37	(140)
Long-term divorced	.25	.44	(131)
Never married	.16	.37	(116)
Recently separated	.21	.41	(58)
Long-term separated	.19	.40	(53)
Remarried throughout	.12	.32	(152)
Remarried, divorced after 1967	.13	.34	(55)
Remarried, divorced in 1967	.19	.39	(43)
Other	.17	.38	(348)
Total, all cases	.16	.36	(2,397)

(1967 data not available)

c. JOB INSECURITY, CURRENT JOB

Marital History	1967 Mean	1967 Standard Deviation	1967 (Number)	1977 Mean	1977 Standard Deviation	1977 (Number)
Married throughout	1.59	.18	(982)	1.57	.18	(1,253)
Recently divorced	1.55	.16	(91)	1.54	.14	(133)
Long-term divorced	1.61	.17	(134)	1.60	.16	(126)
Never married	1.55	.16	(119)	1.57	.15	(111)
Recently separated	1.61	.20	(52)	1.60	.19	(56)
Long-term separated	1.68	.18	(59)	1.69	.17	(51)
Remarried throughout	1.60	.17	(147)	1.58	.15	(149)
Remarried, divorced after 1967	1.58	.17	(42)	1.58	.18	(54)
Remarried, divorced in 1967	1.58	.19	(60)	1.59	.19	(40)
Other	1.61	.18	(336)	1.60	.17	(342)
Total, all cases	1.59	.18	(2,022)	1.58	.17	(2,315)

(Continued on next page)

TABLE C–3—*Continued*

d. SUPERVISORY STATUS, CURRENT JOB

	Year					
	1967			1977		
Marital History	Mean	Standard Deviation	(Number)	Mean	Standard Deviation	(Number)
Married throughout	.28	.20	(984)	.31	.21	(1,260)
Recently divorced	.29	.20	(91)	.30	.19	(133)
Long-term divorced	.22	.18	(135)	.29	.20	(126)
Never married	.30	.21	(119)	.32	.20	(111)
Recently separated	.24	.17	(52)	.27	.18	(56)
Long-term separated	.23	.14	(60)	.24	.14	(51)
Remarried throughout	.24	.19	(148)	.29	.21	(149)
Remarried, divorced after 1967	.28	.28	(42)	.27	.18	(54)
Remarried, divorced in 1967	.26	.19	(60)	.24	.14	(40)
Other	.26	.20	(337)	.28	.20	(343)
Total, all cases	.27	.20	(2,028)	.30	.20	(2,323)

e. FIRM SIZE, CURRENT JOB

	Year 1977		
Marital History	Mean	Standard Deviation	(Number)
Married throughout	374	485	(1,209)
Recently divorced	503	527	(130)
Long-term divorced	491	500	(122)
Never married	546	534	(107)
Recently separated	435	492	(51)
Long-term separated	371	479	(49)
Remarried throughout	338	447	(138)
Remarried, divorced after 1967	392	535	(47)
Remarried, divorced in 1967	397	496	(40)
Other	436	498	(314)
Total, all cases	405	494	(2,207)

(1967 data not available)

(Continued on next page)

TABLE C–3—*Continued*

f. CORE INDUSTRY, CURRENT JOB (dichotomous)

	Year					
	1967			1977		
Marital History	Mean	Standard Deviation	(Number)	Mean	Standard Deviation	(Number)
Married throughout	.30	.46	(997)	.32	.47	(1,291)
Recently divorced	.33	.47	(94)	.40	.49	(140)
Long-term divorced	.39	.49	(136)	.40	.49	(129)
Never married	.36	.48	(121)	.38	.49	(115)
Recently separated	.30	.46	(53)	.45	.50	(58)
Long-term separated	.13	.34	(60)	.11	.32	(53)
Remarried throughout	.33	.47	(148)	.37	.48	(151)
Remarried, divorced after 1967	.35	.48	(43)	.34	.48	(55)
Remarried, divorced in 1967	.37	.49	(60)	.40	.49	(43)
Other	.24	.42	(343)	.32	.47	(346)
Total, all cases	.30	.46	(2,055)	.34	.47	(2,381)

TABLE C–4: *Human Capital Variables*

a. EDUCATION

	Year					
	1967			1977		
Marital History	Mean	Standard Deviation	(Number)	Mean	Standard Deviation	(Number)
Married throughout	11.4	2.6	(2,271)	11.8	2.6	(2,232)
Recently divorced	11.4	2.8	(171)	11.8	2.9	(171)
Long-term divorced	10.6	2.8	(170)	11.4	2.8	(166)
Never married	11.4	3.6	(160)	11.6	3.9	(159)
Recently separated	9.9	2.9	(101)	10.4	2.8	(99)
Long-term separated	8.7	3.1	(84)	9.5	3.3	(82)
Remarried throughout	10.2	2.6	(267)	10.8	2.5	(262)
Remarried, divorced after 1967	10.7	2.3	(81)	11.6	2.1	(79)
Remarried, divorced in 1967	10.5	2.3	(75)	10.9	2.4	(75)
Other	10.0	3.1	(570)	10.6	3.1	(558)
Total, all cases	11.0	2.8	(3,950)	11.4	2.8	(3,883)

(Continued on next page)

TABLE C–4—*Continued*

b. YEARS SINCE SCHOOL

Marital History	Year 1977		
	Mean	Standard Deviation	(Number)
Married throughout	30.4	5.5	(2,271)
Recently divorced	30.0	5.6	(171)
Long-term divorced	31.2	5.3	(170)
Never married	29.7	5.6	(160)
Recently separated	29.5	4.9	(101)
Long-term separated	32.8	5.8	(84)
Remarried throughout	32.1	5.3	(267)
Remarried, divorced after 1967	29.4	5.1	(81)
Remarried, divorced in 1967	30.8	4.4	(75)
Other	33.1	5.5	(570)
Total, all cases	30.9	5.5	(3,950)

(1967 data not calculated)

c. YEARS OF WORK EXPERIENCE

Marital History	Year					
	1967			1977		
	Mean	Standard Deviation	(Number)	Mean	Standard Deviation	(Number)
Married throughout	7.9	6.7	(2,058)	12.4	8.3	(1,886)
Recently divorced	9.0	7.3	(164)	15.4	8.5	(149)
Long-term divorced	11.1	7.1	(162)	17.2	8.4	(153)
Never married	12.9	8.2	(157)	20.7	9.0	(136)
Recently separated	7.8	6.2	(95)	12.7	7.4	(87)
Long-term separated	13.5	8.4	(82)	19.0	10.1	(76)
Remarried throughout	10.4	7.5	(244)	14.9	9.1	(232)
Remarried, divorced after 1967	7.6	5.9	(75)	12.9	7.0	(71)
Remarried, divorced in 1967	12.2	6.2	(73)	17.3	7.5	(71)
Other	10.3	7.8	(527)	15.2	9.3	(469)
Total, all cases	9.0	7.2	(3,637)	13.9	8.8	(3,330)

(Continued on next page)

TABLE C–4—*Continued*

d. YEARS AT CURRENT JOB

	Year					
	1967			1977		
Marital History	Mean	Standard Deviation	(Number)	Mean	Standard Deviation	(Number)
Married throughout	4.9	5.4	(902)	6.4	6.3	(1,071)
Recently divorced	4.3	5.1	(87)	5.5	5.4	(125)
Long-term divorced	4.2	4.6	(124)	7.7	7.0	(113)
Never married	8.6	6.6	(109)	10.3	8.7	(106)
Recently separated	3.3	4.7	(46)	4.9	3.9	(48)
Long-term separated	5.6	6.4	(54)	7.2	6.6	(46)
Remarried throughout	4.8	5.4	(131)	6.4	6.4	(131)
Remarried, divorced after 1967	3.4	5.0	(36)	5.1	6.2	(46)
Remarried, divorced in 1967	4.3	4.3	(53)	5.7	6.2	(39)
Other	5.5	6.0	(297)	6.4	6.5	(281)
Total, all cases	5.0	5.6	(1,839)	6.6	6.5	(2,006)

e. RECEIVED OCCUPATIONAL TRAINING (dichotomous)

	Year					
	1967			1977		
Marital History	Mean	Standard Deviation	(Number)	Mean	Standard Deviation	(Number)
Married throughout	.21	.41	(2,018)	.47	.50	(1,863)
Recently divorced	.25	.44	(151)	.64	.48	(137)
Long-term divorced	.34	.47	(158)	.61	.49	(141)
Never married	.27	.44	(154)	.63	.48	(133)
Recently separated	.14	.35	(90)	.45	.50	(85)
Long-term separated	.12	.33	(82)	.38	.49	(71)
Remarried throughout	.25	.43	(237)	.46	.50	(225)
Remarried, divorced after 1967	.24	.43	(74)	.66	.48	(70)
Remarried, divorced in 1967	.27	.45	(73)	.54	.50	(66)
Other	.20	.40	(518)	.42	.49	(421)
Total, all cases	.22	.41	(3,555)	.49	.50	(3,212)

(Continued on next page)

TABLE C–4—*Continued*

f. OCCUPATIONAL STATUS, CURRENT JOB

		Year				
		1967			1977	
Marital History	Mean	Standard Deviation	(Number)	Mean	Standard Deviation	(Number)
Married throughout	43.2	17.5	(958)	46.1	16.5	(1,217)
Recently divorced	44.9	18.3	(90)	48.4	16.6	(133)
Long-term divorced	41.2	15.5	(130)	45.6	15.9	(122)
Never married	50.1	19.5	(112)	51.2	18.6	(112)
Recently separated	34.5	18.5	(47)	40.8	16.1	(51)
Long-term separated	28.9	13.2	(53)	33.5	18.2	(48)
Remarried throughout	38.7	15.1	(141)	40.4	14.9	(140)
Remarried, divorced after 1967	42.6	12.8	(38)	44.4	15.4	(49)
Remarried, divorced in 1967	39.9	14.4	(56)	42.4	14.7	(42)
Other	36.8	16.2	(324)	40.9	15.8	(326)
Total, all cases	41.4	17.4	(1,949)	44.9	16.6	(2,240)

TABLE C–5: *Family Role Variables*

a. ANY OTHER EARNERS IN HOUSEHOLD (dichotomous)

		Year				
		1966			1976	
Marital History	Mean	Standard Deviation	(Number)	Mean	Standard Deviation	(Number)
Married throughout	.84	.37	(2,273)	.80	.40	(2,121)
Recently divorced	.84	.36	(172)	.31	.46	(172)
Long-term divorced	.26	.44	(170)	.28	.45	(168)
Never married	.20	.40	(164)	.11	.31	(163)
Recently separated	.88	.32	(101)	.35	.48	(99)
Long-term separated	.40	.49	(84)	.33	.47	(81)
Remarried throughout	.86	.35	(267)	.78	.42	(254)
Remarried, divorced after 1967	.81	.39	(81)	.75	.44	(76)
Remarried, divorced in 1967	.26	.44	(76)	.68	.47	(71)
Other	.67	.47	(572)	.47	.50	(543)
Total, all cases	.75	.44	(3,960)	.65	.42	(3,748)

(Continued on next page)

TABLE C–5—*Continued*

b. EARNINGS OF OTHER HOUSEHOLD MEMBERS

	Year					
	1966			1976		
Marital History	Mean	Standard Deviation	(Number)	Mean	Standard Deviation	(Number)
Married throughout	6,400	5,000	(2,273)	12,600	10,800	(2,121)
Recently divorced	6,100	6,200	(172)	1,200	3,300	(172)
Long-term divorced	600	1,400	(170)	1,400	3,300	(168)
Never married	700	1,700	(164)	500	2,000	(163)
Recently separated	4,600	3,600	(101)	1,300	3,500	(99)
Long-term separated	300	800	(84)	1,000	2,700	(81)
Remarried throughout	5,800	4,200	(267)	11,200	10,600	(254)
Remarried, divorced after 1967	5,600	4,200	(81)	10,900	10,100	(76)
Remarried, divorced in 1967	400	1,400	(76)	8,200	8,200	(71)
Other	3,400	4,100	(572)	4,300	7,400	(543)
Total, all cases	5,100	4,900	(3,960)	9,100	10,450	(3,748)

c. HOURS WORKED BY OTHER HOUSEHOLD MEMBERS

	Year					
	1966			1976		
Marital History	Mean	Standard Deviation	(Number)	Mean	Standard Deviation	(Number)
Married throughout	2,400	1,000	(2,273)	2,700	1,600	(2,271)
Recently divorced	2,200	1,000	(172)	600	1,200	(172)
Long-term divorced	600	1,000	(170)	700	1,200	(170)
Never married	800	1,400	(164)	400	1,000	(164)
Recently separated	2,100	900	(101)	500	900	(101)
Long-term separated	500	1,300	(84)	900	1,700	(84)
Remarried throughout	2,300	1,000	(267)	2,200	1,400	(267)
Remarried, divorced after 1967	2,400	1,300	(81)	2,600	1,300	(81)
Remarried, divorced in 1967	300	900	(76)	2,000	1,200	(76)
Other	1,600	1,400	(572)	1,300	1,600	(572)
Total, all cases	2,100	1,200	(3,960)	2,100	1,700	(3,958)

(Continued on next page)

TABLE C–5—*Continued*

d. EGALITARIAN GENDER ATTITUDES

	Year 1977		
Marital History	Mean	Standard Deviation	(Number)
Married throughout	13.4	3.4	(2,238)
Recently divorced	14.3	3.3	(171)
Long-term divorced	13.8	3.4	(168)
Never married	13.5	3.4	(148)
Recently separated	13.0	3.4	(96)
Long-term separated	12.3	3.2	(82)
Remarried throughout	13.2	3.7	(261)
Remarried, divorced after 1967	13.5	3.5	(81)
Remarried, divorced in 1967	13.4	3.4	(76)
Other	12.9	3.5	(553)
Total, all cases	13.3	3.4	(3,874)

(1967 data not available)

e. ANY CHILDREN IN HOUSEHOLD (dichotomous)

	Year					
	1967			1977		
Marital History	Mean	Standard Deviation	(Number)	Mean	Standard Deviation	(Number)
Married throughout	.90	.30	(2,273)	.56	.50	(2,273)
Recently divorced	.87	.34	(172)	.57	.50	(172)
Long-term divorced	.79	.40	(170)	.35	.48	(170)
Never married	.19	.39	(164)	.17	.38	(164)
Recently separated	.90	.30	(101)	.64	.48	(101)
Long-term separated	.81	.40	(84)	.48	.50	(84)
Remarried throughout	.78	.41	(267)	.48	.50	(267)
Remarried, divorced after 1967	.91	.28	(81)	.47	.50	(81)
Remarried, divorced in 1967	.80	.40	(76)	.46	.50	(76)
Other	.78	.41	(572)	.45	.50	(572)
Total, all cases	.83	.37	(3,960)	.51	.49	(3,960)

(Continued on next page)

TABLE C–5—*Continued*

f. NUMBER OF CHILDREN IN HOUSEHOLD

	Year					
	1967			1977		
Marital History	Mean	Standard Deviation	(Number)	Mean	Standard Deviation	(Number)
Married throughout	2.8	1.9	(2,273)	1.2	1.4	(2,273)
Recently divorced	2.9	2.0	(172)	1.1	1.3	(172)
Long-term divorced	2.2	1.9	(170)	0.7	1.2	(170)
Never married	0.6	1.5	(164)	0.4	0.9	(164)
Recently separated	3.9	2.7	(101)	1.9	2.1	(101)
Long-term separated	3.1	2.5	(84)	1.2	1.6	(84)
Remarried throughout	2.3	1.9	(267)	1.0	1.2	(267)
Remarried, divorced after 1967	2.6	1.8	(81)	1.0	1.6	(81)
Remarried, divorced in 1967	2.2	2.1	(76)	1.0	1.4	(76)
Other	2.6	2.3	(572)	0.9	1.4	(572)
Total, all cases	2.6	2.1	(3,960)	1.1	1.4	(3,960)

g. ANY CHILDREN IN HOUSEHOLD UNDER AGE 5 (dichotomous)

	Year					
	1967			1977		
Marital History	Mean	Standard Deviation	(Number)	Mean	Standard Deviation	(Number)
Married throughout	.43	.50	(2,273)	.02	.14	(2,273)
Recently divorced	.46	.50	(172)	.00	.00	(172)
Long-term divorced	.20	.40	(170)	.01	.11	(170)
Never married	.12	.33	(164)	.02	.13	(164)
Recently separated	.53	.50	(101)	.03	.17	(101)
Long-term separated	.33	.47	(84)	.02	.15	(84)
Remarried throughout	.40	.49	(267)	.02	.15	(267)
Remarried, divorced after 1967	.38	.49	(81)	.02	.16	(81)
Remarried, divorced in 1967	.24	.43	(76)	.01	.11	(76)
Other	.31	.46	(572)	.02	.15	(572)
Total, all cases	.38	.49	(3,960)	.02	.14	(3,960)

(Continued on next page)

TABLE C–5 — *Continued*

h. NUMBER OF CHILDREN IN HOUSEHOLD UNDER AGE 5

		Year				
		1967			1977	
Marital History	Mean	Standard Deviation	(Number)	Mean	Standard Deviation	(Number)
Married throughout	.65	.91	(2,273)	.02	.18	(2,273)
Recently divorced	.67	.86	(172)	.00	.00	(172)
Long-term divorced	.34	.77	(170)	.02	.17	(170)
Never married	.21	.60	(164)	.02	.19	(164)
Recently separated	1.15	1.34	(101)	.06	.37	(101)
Long-term separated	.61	1.03	(84)	.02	.15	(84)
Remarried throughout	.58	.85	(267)	.03	.23	(267)
Remarried, divorced after 1967	.57	.91	(81)	.02	.16	(81)
Remarried, divorced in 1967	.34	.72	(76)	.01	.11	(76)
Other	.49	.87	(572)	.03	.17	(572)
Total, all cases	.60	.90	(3,960)	.02	.18	(3,960)

i. TOTAL FERTILITY

	Year 1977		
Marital History	Mean	Standard Deviation	(Number)
Married throughout	3.5	2.3	(2,273)
Recently divorced	3.5	2.5	(172)
Long-term divorced	3.2	2.4	(170)
Never married	0.9	2.0	(164)
Recently separated	4.7	3.2	(101)
Long-term separated	4.4	3.2	(84)
Remarried throughout	3.3	2.4	(267)
Remarried, divorced after 1967	3.5	2.4	(81)
Remarried, divorced in 1967	3.4	2.3	(76)
Other	3.5	2.9	(572)
Total, all cases	3.4	2.5	(3,960)

(1967 data not calculated)

(Continued on next page)

TABLE C–5—*Continued*

j.   AGE

| | Year 1977 | | |
| | | Standard | |
Marital History	Mean	Deviation	(Number)
Married throughout	47.9	4.4	(2,273)
Recently divorced	47.4	4.4	(172)
Long-term divorced	47.8	4.4	(170)
Never married	47.2	4.3	(164)
Recently separated	45.4	3.8	(101)
Long-term separated	47.4	4.5	(84)
Remarried throughout	48.2	4.4	(267)
Remarried, divorced after 1967	46.1	4.3	(81)
Remarried, divorced in 1967	47.3	4.4	(76)
Other	49.1	4.3	(572)
Total, all cases	47.9	4.4	(3,960)

(1967 data not calculated)

TABLE C–6:   *Work Orientation*

| | 1967 | | | | |
	Homemaker	Intermittent Worker	Career Woman	TOTAL[a]	(Number)
Married throughout	31%	53%	15%	100%	(1,933)
Recently divorced	23%	52%	25%	100%	(156)
Long-term divorced	17%	54%	29%	100%	(160)
Never married	13%	22%	66%	100%	(143)
Recently separated	27%	51%	22%	100%	(88)
Long-term separated	12%	42%	45%	100%	(80)
Remarried throughout	23%	54%	23%	100%	(235)
Remarried, divorced after 1967	27%	59%	14%	100%	(71)
Remarried, divorced in 1967	12%	56%	32%	100%	(72)
Other	24%	52%	24%	100%	(497)
Total, all cases	27%	52%	21%	100%	(3,435)

[a] Percentages may not total 100% due to rounding.

APPENDIX D

Corrections for Selection Bias

D.1 SELECTION BIAS WITH RESPECT TO LABOR FORCE PARTICIPATION

The corrections for selection bias used in Chapters 4 and 5 require the development of models to predict the probability of working for each respondent. Two such models were estimated using the SAS LOGIST procedure (Harrell 1985). The first model predicts the probability of working during 1976. This predicted probability of working was then used as the correction for selection bias in the analyses of annual hours in 1976 (Table 4-2) and annual earnings in 1976 (Table 5-1). The second model predicts the probability of working at the time of the 1977 interview. This predicted probability is used as the correction for selection bias in the analysis of hourly wage at current job in 1977 (Table 5-2).

The model used to predict the probability of working during 1976 is similar to that presented in Chapter 4 (Table 4-1), except that the marital history variables are not included as predictors (see Table D-1). The variables measuring years since school, which are statistically significant in the model including the marital history variables (Table 4-1), are not statistically significant in this model (Table D-1). Nevertheless, they are retained in the model for theoretical reasons. (Descriptive statistics for the correction for selection bias derived from this equation are provided in Table D-2.)

The model used to predict the probability of working at the time of the interview in 1977 uses a somewhat different set of predictors than the model predicting the probability of working during 1976 (see Table D-3). Hours worked by others in the household has the expected negative effect; age has a positive effect, but at a declining rate. Earnings of other household members have a positive effect on the probability of working. Reasons for this unexpected finding are discussed in Chapter 4. (Descriptive statistics for the correction for selection bias derived from this equation are provided in Table D-4.)

D.2 SELECTION BIAS WITH RESPECT TO MARITAL HISTORY

As noted in Chapter 4, other types of selection bias might also affect the analyses

TABLE D–1:

Predictive Model of Labor Force Participation in 1976

Independent Variables	Dependent Variable Labor Force Participation, 1976 (N = 3,613) Logistic Regression Coefficients (standard error in parentheses)
Nonwhite	.37*** (.08)
Education	.05*** (.02)
Years since school	.04 (.06)
Years since school, squared	− .001 (.001)
Earnings of other household members (Ln)	− .005 (.008)
Egalitarian gender attitudes	.14*** (.01)
Number of children	− .20*** (.03)
Chi-square degrees of freedom	363.25*** (7)

Ln = Natural logarithm transformation.
*** $p < .001$

of labor force status, hours, earnings and wages. Prior work or family factors may affect both women's marital history and their work outcomes. If this is the case, marital history effects on work outcomes will appear to be stronger than they actually are, when in fact prior work/family factors have affected both marital history and work outcomes. Therefore, several selection processes affecting marital history must be considered. Currently divorced women first married, then divorced, and did not remarry (see Glass et al. 1983). To control for the effects of these selection processes, models were developed predicting the probability of marriage for all women, the probability of divorce after 1967 for women married in 1967, and the probability of remarriage after 1967 for women divorced in 1967.

The model predicting probability of marriage is relatively weak, since few variables were available for inclusion in the model (not shown). Nonwhite and highly educated women are less likely to marry, while older women are more likely to be married.

TABLE D–2:

Predicted Probability of Working in 1976, by Marital History

Marital History	Mean	Standard Deviation	(Number)
I. All Cases			
Married throughout	.58	.15	(2,059)
Recently divorced	.63	.15	(170)
Long-term divorced	.63	.15	(162)
Never married	.66	.15	(142)
Other marital history	.58	.16	(1,078)
Total, all cases	.59	.15	(3,611)
II. Cases in Table 4–2			
Married throughout	.64	.13	(807)
Recently divorced	.66	.13	(109)
Long-term divorced	.65	.15	(97)
Never married	.68	.13	(86)
Other marital history	.62	.14	(464)
Total, cases in Table 4–2	.64	.13	(1,563)
III. Cases in Table 5–1			
Married throughout	.63	.13	(895)
Recently divorced	.66	.13	(113)
Long-term divorced	.66	.15	(99)
Never married	.68	.13	(92)
Other marital history	.61	.14	(504)
Total, cases in Table 5–1	.63	.14	(1,703)

The model predicting probability of divorce is consistent with other research in this area (Mott and Moore 1979, Huber and Spitze 1981, Booth and Edwards 1985, South and Spitze 1986, Bianchi and Spain 1986). Older women, women who married later, and women who have young children are less likely to divorce than other women. Nonwhite women and those who have greater work experience are more likely to divorce.

The probability of remarriage is also affected by work and family characteristics (Bianchi and Spain 1986). Nonwhite women are less likely to remarry, as are older women. While years since divorce was expected to have a strong positive effect on likelihood of remarriage (see Cherlin 1981), its effect was not statistically significant, nor was there a significant curvilinear relationship between the two variables. Years of education and work experience have a positive effect on the likelihood that a woman would have remarried. While this finding may at first seem surprising, since

TABLE D–3:

Predictive Model of Labor Force Participation in 1977

Independent Variables	Dependent Variable Labor Force Participation, 1977 (N = 3,682) Logistic Regression Coefficients (standard error in parentheses)
Nonwhite	.52*** (.08)
Education	.13*** (.01)
Earnings of other household members (Ln)	.04*** (.01)
Hours worked by other household members	− .0001*** (.00002)
Total fertility	− .06*** (.02)
Any children	− .22** (.09)
Age	.42** (.18)
Age, squared	− .005** (.002)
Chi-square degrees of freedom	221.90*** (8)

Ln = Natural logarithm transformation.

** p < .01

*** p < .001

these women presumably have fewer economic incentives to remarry, work experience and perhaps education may increase a woman's chances of meeting potential spouses and may make her more attractive in the (re)marriage market (Peters 1986). Although children are hypothesized to provide an incentive to remarry, no statistically significant effect is identified for any of the measures (presence, number, total fertility) tested here. Perhaps having children makes a divorced woman less desirable to a potential spouse.

The predicted probabilities of marriage, divorce and remarriage were added to each of the equations for labor force status (Table 4-1), hours worked (Table 4-2), annual earnings (Table 5-1), and hourly wages (Table 5-2) as corrections for selection

TABLE D–4:

Predicted Probability of Working in 1977, by Marital History

Marital History	Mean	Standard Deviation	(Number)
I. All Cases			
Married throughout	.50	.12	(2,083)
Recently divorced	.53	.12	(171)
Long-term divorced	.55	.13	(164)
Never married	.58	.13	(158)
Other marital history	.51	.12	(1,102)
Total, all cases	.51	.12	(3,678)
II. Cases in Table 5–2			
Married throughout	.53	.11	(774)
Recently divorced	.56	.12	(101)
Long-term divorced	.58	.12	(92)
Never married	.62	.10	(80)
Other marital history	.53	.11	(436)
Total, cases in Table 5–2	.54	.11	(1,483)

bias. These tests were run using the models in column 1 of Table 4-1 and in column 2 of each of the other tables, i.e., after controlling for the effects of the correction for the probability of working. (Never-married women were excluded from models controlling for the predicted probability of divorce; women who never divorced were excluded from models controlling for the predicted probability of remarriage.) In some cases, the correction's effects on the dependent variable were not statistically significant. In all cases, the inclusion of the correction in the equation did not significantly alter the coefficients for the marital history variables. Therefore, the conclusions regarding the effects of marital history on each of these dependent variables are essentially the same whether or not these corrections for selection bias are included in the models. The only correction for selection bias that has an independent effect on the results is the correction for probability of working, which has been included in the models for hours, earnings, and wages.

NOTES

CHAPTER 1

1. Weitzman 1985, p. 339.

2. Norton and Moorman 1987.

3. Plateris 1979, U.S. Bureau of the Census 1985a.

4. Cherlin 1981.

5. See Espenshade 1985 and U.S. Bureau of the Census 1985a. Although remarriage rates have decreased, a majority of women whose first marriage ends in divorce are remarried five years after the divorce (U.S. Bureau of the Census 1976, Espenshade 1985, Norton and Moorman 1987).

6. U.S. Bureau of the Census 1967, 1985b.

7. Treiman and Hartman 1981, Beller 1984.

8. Bianchi and Spain 1986, p. 170; see also Pear 1983 and O'Neill 1985.

9. Pear 1984.

10. Greene and Quester (1982) have argued that this increasing risk of divorce has raised the labor force participation rates of married women.

11. Kanter 1977b, p. 8. See also Sokoloff 1980, Oppenheimer 1982.

12. Smith 1979, U.S. Bureau of the Census 1980, U.S. Bureau of Labor Statistics 1981, 1983, 1984.

13. U.S. Bureau of the Census 1970, U.S. Bureau of Labor Statistics 1980.

14. Beller 1984, Beller and Han 1984.

15. Waite 1978.

16. Thornton et al. 1983.

17. Cherlin 1980, Dowd 1983.

18. It should be noted that alimony and child support awards before the

146

enactment of no-fault divorce laws were also inadequate. It is not clear to what extent inadequate awards are the result of no-fault divorce laws per se.

19. Weitzman 1985, p. 339.

20. Weitzman, 1985, p. 355.

21. See, for example, Hoffman 1977, Weiss 1984.

22. Corcoran 1979b.

23. Espenshade 1979.

24. Shaw 1978, Corcoran 1979b, Espenshade 1979, Bianchi and Spain 1986.

25. Shaw 1978.

26. Moore 1979.

27. Weitzman 1985, p. 343.

28. See also Hoffman 1977.

29. Hampton 1975, Hoffman and Holmes 1976, Hoffman 1977, Corcoran 1979b, Bianchi and Spain 1986.

30. Shaw 1978, p. 193.

31. The category "currently married women" includes women who have been married only once and married women who have remarried after divorce or widowhood. "Formerly married women" includes separated women, divorced women, and widowed women. Several other categories of women are referred to in the following discussion. "Ever-divorced women" include currently divorced women and women who have remarried after a divorce. "Married, never-divorced women" are women who are currently married and have never divorced. "Single women" are women who are currently divorced, separated, widowed, or who have never been married. ("Separated women" are considered to be single even though they are still technically married). Ever-married women are all women defined previously as currently married or formerly married.

32. See, for example, Mincer and Polachek 1974, Treiman and Terrell 1975, Hudis 1976, Hill 1979.

33. Hudis 1976.

34. Haurin 1986. See also Shaw 1978, who presents data for formerly married women.

35. Moore 1979.

36. Nestel et al. 1983.

37. Roos 1983, p. 853.

38. Roos 1983.

39. Suter and Miller 1973, Mincer and Polachek 1974, Treiman and Terrell 1975, Hudis 1976, Roos 1985.

40. Treiman and Terrell 1975, Roos 1983, 1985.

41. Oppenheimer 1970, p. 136. This shift was accelerated by legislation prohibiting discrimination on the basis of marital status. Federal statutes, 42 USC §200e–1 et al., have been interpreted by case law to forbid employment practices that deny one sex the right to exercise fundamental human rights that are granted to the other (e.g., hiring married men, but not married women). See *Planchet v. New Hampshire Hospital,* 1975, 341 A.2d 267. In addition, a number of states have enacted legislation which explicitly establishes as an unlawful discriminatory practice the refusal to hire, or the discharge of, an individual because of his/her marital status (e.g., N.Y. Human Rights Law Sec. 296).

42. Malkiel and Malkiel 1973, Halaby 1979.

43. Hyman 1983, Bianchi and Spain 1986.

44. Sweet (1973) has argued that remarried women are more attached to the labor market than women in their first marriage, since remarried women want to be prepared to support themselves if they again experience marital disruption. See also Oppenheimer 1982.

45. See discussion of research findings by Salvo and McNeil 1984, above.

46. See, for example, Hanson 1983.

47. Mincer and Polachek 1974, Killingsworth 1983.

48. Blau and Duncan 1967.

49. Becker 1975.

50. See Sokoloff 1980, p. 20, and Treiman and Hartmann 1981, p. 17, for further elaboration of these assumptions. Hauser (1980) argues that recent stratification research has not made these assumptions, and has questioned the competitiveness and homogeneity of the labor market. Knottnerus (1987) argues that the assumptions of status attainment theory are also drawn from an image of modern society based on universalism.

51. DeJong et al. 1971, Treiman and Terrell 1975, Featherman and Hauser 1976, McClendon 1976.

52. Featherman and Hauser 1976.

53. Bose and Rossi 1983, Roos 1983, 1985.

54. Featherman and Hauser 1976.

55. Becker 1981, p. 21.

56. See discussion by Mortimer et al. (1978) of the "two-person" career; also Pfeffer and Ross 1982.

57. See Becker 1975 for a full discussion of human capital theory. For a review of human capital research, see Bianchi and Spain 1986, pp. 188–195.

58. See also Darian 1975, Treiman and Terrell 1975.

59. Polachek 1975.

60. Hudis 1976, Hill 1979.

61. See also the discussion in Bianchi and Spain 1986, pp. 157–159.

62. See, for example, critiques by Sandell and Shapiro 1978, Corcoran 1979a, Corcoran and Duncan 1979.

63. Hanson 1983.

64. See also Killingsworth (1983, pp. 29–38) for a discussion of family labor supply models.

65. Macke et al. 1978, Thornton et al. 1983.

66. Beck et al. 1978, Tolbert et al. 1980, Wanner and Lewis 1983.

67. Stolzenberg 1978.

68. Stolzenberg 1978.

69. Doeringer and Piore 1971, Baron and Bielby 1980, Sorenson 1983.

70. See Bibb and Form 1977, Beck et al. 1978, Tolbert et al. 1980, and Treiman and Hartmann 1981, among others, for a discussion of distinctions between the core and periphery industries. Dual labor market theory is closely related to the dual economy theory, although there are theoretical distinctions (Wallace and Kalleberg 1981).

71. Treiman and Hartmann 1981, p. 47.

72. Medoff and Abraham 1980, 1981.

73. Hirsch 1980.

74. Baron and Bielby 1980, Hirsch 1980.

75. Blau and Jusenius 1976, Kanter 1977a, Baron and Bielby 1980, Rosenbaum 1984.

76. Stolzenberg 1978, Sorensen 1983, Hodson 1984.

77. See Baron and Bielby 1980, 1984, Hirsch 1980, Sorenson 1983. Even among those who view the firm as an important structural variable, with a concomitant emphasis on *jobs;* there is a recognition that *occupations* are in some cases also the locus of mobility processes (Spilerman 1977, Baron and Bielby 1980,

Wanner and Lewis 1983). In some occupations (e.g., crafts, professions) mobility occurs primarily *between* firms and "work performance is regulated by professional norms" (Baron and Bielby 1980, p. 739).

78. In fact, earnings are viewed as a characteristic of jobs, not people (Sorenson 1983). Note that, to avoid tautology, jobs or other labor market segments must not be defined by wage rates.

79. See discussion in Chapter 4, Section 5.

80. Coverman 1983.

81. See also Coverman 1986.

82. There is some question about whether being in a union job has a positive effect on women's earnings, since many unionized women are in highly sex-segregated jobs. Bibb and Form (1977) found that while the bivariate correlation between earnings and being a union member was positive, the effect of union membership on women's earnings was slightly negative after controlling for other segmentation and human capital variables.

83. See also Blau and Jusenius 1976, Bielby and Baron 1986.

84. Bibb and Form 1977.

85. Stolzenberg 1978.

86. Hodson 1984, Coverman 1986.

87. Bibb and Form 1977.

88. Bielby and Baron 1984.

89. See also Tolbert et al. 1980.

90. See also Hodson 1984, who found an even wider gap in percentage female between the core and periphery sectors, and Coverman 1986.

91. Hauser (1980), in his re-analysis of Beck et al. (1978), found a significant negative effect of being female in both the core and periphery sectors. This effect was slightly (but not significantly) stronger in the periphery sector. In their reply, Beck et al. (1980) used different data (the 1976 Current Population Survey) and found a negative effect of being female on earnings in both sectors. However, this negative effect was significantly stronger in the core sector. Further details of this analysis are presented in Tolbert et al. (1980).

92. Sorenson 1983.

93. An alternative test of the effects of women's family obligations would focus on the effects of children on women's careers. Waite et al. (1985) argue that it is parenthood, and not marriage by itself, that disadvantages women in the labor market. In the present study, the vast majority of ever-married women have had children; the distinction between marriage and parenthood is unlikely to affect the findings.

Furthermore, the effects of children on a woman's career are likely to depend on her marital history. For example, while care of children may actually be more of a burden for working divorced women than for working married women, children represent a much stronger economic incentive for divorced women than for married women (see discussion in Chapter 7). For a discussion of the effects of parenthood on women's labor force behavior, see Waite et al. (1985).

CHAPTER 2

1. Perrucci 1978, Hanson 1983.

2. The argument here is not that age variation is unimportant in this sample, but that it is less important than it would be in a sample that included adult women of all ages. See Mott (1978, p. 23) for a discussion of age variation within the sample.

3. Parnes et al. 1976.

4. Rhoton 1984, p. 12.

5. Carmines and Zeller 1979.

6. Hyman 1983, Bianchi and Spain 1986.

7. It is, for example, logically impossible to be remarried in 1967 and never married in 1977.

8. Women who married for the first time during the survey period would, of course, be of great interest in this study. A first marriage is the most significant and frequent marital status change for most people. However, only thirty-eight women in the sample married for the first time during the survey period; hence a separate analysis of this group was precluded.

9. There is some evidence of such remarriages and divorces in the intervening years for the following numbers of women in each marital history group (percentages represent percent of total number in each category): recently divorced, 23 (13%); long-term divorced, 23 (13%); recently separated, 7 (7%); long-term separated, 9 (11%); remarried, divorced after 1967, 2 (2%); and remarried, divorced in 1967, 6 (8%).

10. Weiss 1975, p. 21.

11. The remaining 13 cases had missing data at one or more of the intervening interviews.

12. Further details of the weighting procedure are described in Center for Human Resource Research (1981).

13. While blacks were oversampled, controlling for race removes any bias caused by the oversampling. Standard errors are reduced for the oversampled group,

making it more likely that a group difference will be found statistically significant. However, that is the purpose of oversampling—to obtain more reliable tests for the oversampled group. Note also that race increases explained variance artifactually, since racial groups are not represented in their true proportions in the population.

14. Mosteller and Tukey 1977.

15. Tukey 1977, pp. 79–80.

16. Tukey 1977.

17. Cohen and Cohen 1975.

CHAPTER 3

1. Treiman and Terrell 1975, Hudis 1976, Grossman 1977, Lopata and Norr 1980.

2. Shaw 1978, Moore 1979.

3. Hoffman 1977 and Espenshade 1979, are exceptions.

4. See the description of the marital history categories in Chapter 2.

5. The year 1966 was chosen to take advantage of the fact that some of the outcome measures are available for that year, since the 1967 interview asked about hours worked and income received in 1966.

6. See Cohen and Cohen 1975, pp. 219–222.

7. See Appelbaum 1981 and Roos 1983, among others, for a discussion of the reasons for this increase.

8. A separate analysis (not shown) indicates that the 8% increase is about equally due to an aging effect (women return to the labor force as their children grow up and/or leave the household) and to a period effect (the general tendency for women to enter the labor force during the 1970s).

9. This effect is much stronger than the 1 percentage point difference (12% − 11%) found by Corcoran (1979b, p. 350) over a seven-year period using data for women aged 35 through 44 in the Panel Study of Income Dynamics. These different findings may be accounted for by the longer time period considered here, the slight difference in defining age groups, or other differences between the NLS and the Panel Study of Income Dynamics.

10. Hampton 1975, Booth et al. 1984.

11. Moore 1979, Greene and Quester 1982, Arendell 1986.

12. Moore 1979.

13. See Weiss 1975, p. 17 for anecdotal evidence.

14. See Killingsworth 1983, and the discussion of income and substitution effects in Chapter 4, below.

15. "Tastes for work" is a term used by economists to refer to the degree to which people prefer to spend their time in work rather than leisure (see Killingsworth 1983, p. 75).

16. Heckman 1974, p. 679.

17. Note that the dependent variable in Table 3-2, annual hours, is measured in the year prior to the year that marital status was determined (1966 vs. 1967, 1976 vs. 1977). The same is true for the data on annual earnings presented in Table 3-3. However, to the extent that marital status changed in that one-year period, the effect would be to *minimize* differences among the marital history groups. The analyses of hours worked (and annual earnings) were re-run using hours worked in 1967 and marital history based on a 1976 measure of marital status: there were no meaningful differences between those results and the results presented in Tables 3-2 and 3-3. The 1976 measure of marital status did not include a question on number of marriages. For that reason, women who were still married to their first spouse in 1967 and who had divorced and remarried by 1976 could not be distinguished from those who were still married to their first spouse in 1976. Since this measure of marital history is not as refined as the one based on 1977 marital status, since the reference group is different (it includes some remarried women) and since all other results are based on the 1977 measure, the results from the 1976 measure of marital status are not presented here.

18. Sweet 1973, Greene and Quester 1982.

19. Hampton 1975, Hannan et al. 1977, Booth et al. 1984.

20. Note that the wage data presented here (Table 3-4) refer to wage at current job (1967 and 1977), while data on hours worked (Table 3-2) and on annual earnings (Table 3-3) refer to the previous year (1966 and 1976).

21. Comparable data for the U.S. are not readily available; among full-time workers, women experienced a 10% increase and men an 11% increase in real median wage between 1967 and 1977 (U.S. Department of Labor 1980, p. 49).

22. Greene and Quester (1982) found that married women who have a high risk of divorce have slightly higher wages than other married women, even after controlling for the higher labor force participation rate of married women who have a high risk of divorce. However, their data did not permit a comparison of married women who remained married with married women who later divorced.

23. While family income decreases after divorce, some women report that they have greater control over income. See Brown et al. (1976) for a discussion of this issue.

24. The interpretation of Table 3-5 would have been substantially the same if the

income/needs ratio rather than family income had been used as a measure of economic well-being. See Appendix Table C-1.

25. The gap between recently divorced women and continuously married women does widen slightly, up from 3 to 6 percentage points.

26. Note that while most states do not provide public assistance to married women living with their spouses, some states do allow such payments.

27. Weiss 1975, p. 4.

28. See Roos 1985, p. 122, for a discussion of the importance of this issue.

29. This polarization also seems to occur among separated women.

CHAPTER 4

1. Killingsworth 1983, p. 3.

2. No attempt is made to impute a wage for nonworkers, since imputed wages are derived from estimates for workers only. As Killingsworth (1983, p. 93) has pointed out, workers are likely to have higher wages than nonworkers would have if they entered the labor force. This bias would be reflected in any wage imputed to nonworkers.

3. Use of 1977 wage introduces two minor problems. First, there is a discrepancy in the timing of the measures of hours worked (1976) and hourly wage (1977). It is assumed that there is a fairly high correlation between 1976 wage and 1977 wage (the observed correlation is .75), and therefore that the difference in timing of measures does not seriously affect the results. Secondly, not all women who worked in 1976 were working in 1977. Those for whom 1977 wage data are missing are excluded from the analysis of hours worked. The exclusion of these 72 cases is assumed to have minimal effects on the results.

4. Heckman 1979, Berk 1983.

5. Peterson 1987.

6. Coefficients in this logistic regression model can be interpreted as the effect of a one-unit change in the independent variable on the log odds of being employed. Significance levels are determined using the chi-square ststistic. The models were estimated using the SAS Logist Procedure (Harrell 1985).

7. However, the variable "nonwhite" increases chi-square artifactually, since racial groups are not represented in their true proportions in the population.

8. The models in this chapter and in Chapter 5 are concerned with differences among the groups of continuously married women, recently divorced women, long-term divorced women, and never-married women. These four categories are

considered separately in these analyses for the theoretical reasons described in Chapter 1. The remaining marital history groups were combined into the "other marital history" category because they are of less interest in this study, and because differences in labor supply and personal income between these groups and continuously married women were not statistically significant, after controlling for race (data not shown).

9. While the effect of race is not statistically significant, the variable "nonwhite" is retained in the equation to remove the effects of race from the effects of subsequently entered variables.

10. Killingsworth 1983.

11. The coefficient for the "other marital history" group becomes statistically significant at this point. However, since this group is of no particular interest in this study, no further analysis of this effect was conducted and no interpretation is offered.

12. Note that when the marital history variables are excluded from the model, earnings of other household members have a negative, though not statistically significant, effect (see Appendix Table D-1).

13. Killingsworth 1983.

14. Total fertility is the number of children a woman has had, regardless of whether or not they currently live in her household.

15. Floge (1986, p. 18) in an exploratory study of women's search for day care, concludes that "married women have greater child care resources than single women."

16. See Moen (1986) for a discussion of how age of children affects labor force participation of divorced women.

17. Sorenson 1983.

18. Heckman 1979, Berk 1983.

19. Waite and Hudis (1980, p. 112) argue that "behavioral expectations by either workers or employers will affect the actual behaviors of *both* workers and employers" (emphasis in original).

20. Fligstein et al. 1983.

21. It could be argued that the inadequacy of the labor market segmentation variables is due to poor measurement rather than to some theoretical inadequacy.

22. Treiman and Terrell 1975, Roos 1983, 1985.

23. See the description of the procedure for testing interactions at the end of Section 4.3.

24. Hodson (1985) argues that interaction effects are more likely to be statistically significant when logged dependent variables (such as hours worked in this

chapter, and earnings and wages in Chapter 5) are used, rather than untransformed dependent variables. Furthermore, he argues that the direction of interaction effects found with logged dependent variables is often opposite that found with untransformed variables, and is often counter-intuitive. Interactions for the hours equation in this chapter, and for the earnings and wage equations in Chapter 5 were tested with both logged and untransformed dependent variables. In each case, *more* statistically significant interactions were identified with the untransformed variable than with the logged variable. Furthermore, the significant interactions that were identified with logged dependent variables were, for the most part, theoretically plausible. For these reasons, discussion of interaction effects for hours, earnings, and wages refers to tests performed with logged dependent variables.

25. See Killingsworth 1983 for a review of this research.

CHAPTER 5

1. When the dependent variable is expressed as a natural logarithm, the effects can be interpreted as the percentage change in the dependent variable associated with a unit change in the independent variable. If the regression coefficient is sufficiently small (under .25 or so), the regression coefficient itself is a satisfactory estimate of the percentage change, although biased slightly downward. In the results for annual hours, all effects discussed were under .25 (see Table 4-2). Larger regression coefficients are not satisfactory estimates of percentage change, however, as they are severely downwardly biased. In that case, the percentage change is given by a formula, $100e^b - 100$ where e is the base for the natural logarithm and b is the regression coefficient. A coefficient of .56, for example, represents a percentage difference of 75%.

2. See the discussion of this issue in Chapter 4.

3. Number of hours worked per week was also tested, but surprisingly had no effect after controlling for other variables in the model.

4. The latter finding may seem counter-intuitive and may illustrate Hodson's (1985) argument about the problem of testing interactions with logged dependent variables (see Chapter 4, Note 24). However, a test of these interactions using untransformed wages produced interaction effects in the same direction (although they did not quite reach statistical significance). Furthermore, there is some theoretical support for the argument that nonwhite women have higher returns to education than do white women (see Farley 1984).

5. Malkiel and Malkiel 1973, Siebert and Sloane 1981.

6. Hourly wage, rather than annual earnings, was chosen as the dependent variable because annual earnings are strongly affected by annual hours worked. As noted in Chapter 4, variation in hours worked reflects individual choices largely unrelated to labor market segmentation, human capital, or family role variables. Since

hourly wage is not subject to such idiosyncratic factors, it was chosen as the best available measure of demand for labor.

7. Hodson (1985) argues that differences in rates of return should be tested using untransformed dependent variables rather than logged dependent variables. The analyses presented in Table 5-3 were also estimated using untransformed wages. The results are quite similar and do not lead to any different interpretations. For that reason, logged wages are used in Table 5-3 as they were in Table 5-2.

8. Coverman (1983), for example, found that time spent in domestic labor (including child care) has a negative effect on married women's wages. Roos (1985) found that married women who have children are more likely than never-married or married but childless women to be in the lowest-paying occupations.

9. Coverman and Kemp (1987) also conclude that children represent an incentive to work; they found that number of children has a positive effect on hours worked by women who head families.

10. Note that the proportion of variation explained by the earnings and wage models considered here is generally as high as that found in other similar studies. See, for example, Mincer and Polachek 1974, Treiman and Terrell 1975, Featherman and Hauser 1976, Bibb and Form 1977, Perrucci 1978, Corcoran 1979a, Corcoran and Duncan 1979, Tolbert et al. 1980, and Tienda et al. 1987.

CHAPTER 6

1. Elder (1978) has argued that the life-course perspective is concerned with the interplay of social history and life history. Since the NLS data follow a single cohort and cover a narrow age range, the interaction between social history and life history cannot be considered here. The life-course perspective developed here, however, is consistent with the approach described by Elder and Liker (1982, p. 243):

> A life-course perspective on aging assumes that individuals assess and react to new situations in the light of their biographies. The ups and downs of a lifetime furnish lessons, liabilities, and resources that influence the ways in which men and women age and meet the realities of later life.

This approach is broader, in that it includes in a person's biography both individual life history and the interplay between social history and life history. A similar view has recently been expressed by Dannefer (1987) who stresses the importance of "intracohort differentiation over the life course" (p. 211).

2. Lopata and Norr 1980, p. 7.

3. Lopata and Norr 1980, p. 8.

4. See Roos 1985, pp. 120–122.

5. Killingsworth 1983.

6. Racial differences in the effects of variables in each model were tested, but, in each case, the set of interaction terms was not significant (data not shown).

7. As noted in Appendix A, the maximum possible years of work experience during the 10-year study period is 8, since the NLS surveys did not ask about work experience in 1972 or 1974.

8. While age may be an important variable, there is little age variation in this sample.

9. These results reflect the effects of alimony and child support controlling for other variables in the model. However, even at the bivariate level, the correlations between the income/needs ratio and the alimony and child support variables are low — .08 and .07, respectively.

10. Espenshade 1979.

11. Nine women received both alimony and child support, and are counted in both categories.

12. The logistic regression models for poverty status and for public assistance status were estimated using the SAS Logist procedure (Harrell 1985).

13. While it may seem unusual that over one-third of divorced women receiving public assistance are not poor, poverty is defined here on the basis of total family income, including public assistance income. Most of these women would have been poor had they not received public assistance income. Note also that the definition of poverty used here is not exactly the same as that used by the Census Bureau (see discussion in Chapter 3 and Appendix A).

14. Bianchi and Spain 1986.

15. Weitzman 1985.

CHAPTER 7

1. This study was handicapped because measures of some job characteristics had to be imputed from another data set on the basis of occupation. Questions that would help identify specific labor market segments should routinely be included in labor force surveys. Data on labor market segmentation should also be obtained by surveying employers. Information on a variety of organizational characteristics could be obtained (including the racial and gender composition of the work force), along with data about internal processes (number and length of job ladders, divisions, etc.). If these employer data could be linked to employee data, they would provide a valuable resource for analyses of the effects of labor market structure on work outcomes. See Kalleberg (1986) for a proposal to collect employer data and link them with employee data.

2. Since annual earnings reflect the effects of both labor supply (hours worked) and earning power (hourly wage), the explanatory power of the earnings model falls midway between that of the hours and the wage models.

3. See Killingsworth (1983) for a more detailed discussion.

4. See, for example, Hodson 1984, Rosenbaum 1984, Coverman 1986.

5. See, for example, Roos 1985.

6. Siebert and Sloane 1981, p. 128.

7. The availability of detailed monthly panel data from the Survey of Income and Program Participation may enable such an analysis.

8. Weitzman 1985, pp. 205–207.

9. "Average" is defined as the median for the sample as a whole.

10. Arendell's (1986) study, which focused on women who had been divorced 3 to 6 years, found that very few divorced women regained the standard of living they enjoyed during marriage. However, her study is based on a small local sample of women who were middle class during their marriages; the generalizability of her findings is unknown.

11. Moen and Smith 1986.

BIBLIOGRAPHY

Appelbaum, Eileen. 1981. *Back to Work*. Boston: Auburn House.

Arendell, Terry. 1986. *Mothers and Divorce*. Berkeley and Los Angeles: University of California Press.

Baron, James N. and William T. Bielby. 1980. "Bringing the Firms Back in: Stratification, Segmentation, and the Organization of Work." *American Sociological Review* 45:737–765.

_____. 1984. "The Organization of Work in a Segmented Economy." *American Sociological Review* 49:454–473.

Beck, E.M., Patrick Horan, and Charles M. Tolbert II. 1978. "Stratification in a Dual Economy: A Sectoral Model of Earnings Determination." *American Sociological Review* 43:704–720.

_____. 1980. "Social Stratification in Industrial Society: Further Evidence for a Structural Alternative." (Reply to Hauser). *American Sociological Review* 45:712–719.

Becker, Gary S. 1975. *Human Capital*. New York: Columbia University Press.

_____. 1981. *A Treatise on the Family*. Cambridge, MA: Harvard University Press.

Beller, Andrea H. 1984. "Trends in Occupational Segregation by Sex and Race, 1960–1981." Pp. 11–26 in Barbara Reskin (ed.), *Sex Segregation in the Workplace*. Washington, DC: National Academy Press.

_____ and Kee-ok Kim Han. 1984. "Occupational Sex Segregation: Prospects for the 1980's." Pp. 91–114 in Barbara Reskin (ed.), *Sex Segregation in the Workplace*. Washington, DC: National Academy Press.

Berk, Richard. 1983. "An Introduction to Sample Selection Bias in Sociological Data." *American Sociological Review* 48:386–398.

Bianchi, Susan and Daphne Spain. 1986. *American Women in Transition*. New York: Russell Sage Foundation.

Bibb, Robert and William Form. 1977. "The Effects of Industrial, Occupational, and Sex Stratification on Wages in Blue-Collar Markets." *Social Forces* 55:974–996.

Bielby, William and James Baron. 1984. "A Woman's Place is with Other Women: Sex Segregation within Organizations." Pp. 27–55 in Barbara Reskin (ed.), *Sex Segregation in the Workplace*. Washington, DC: National Academy Press.

_____. 1986. "Men and Women at Work: Sex Segregation and Statistical Discrimination." *American Journal of Sociology* 91:759–799.

Blau, Francine D. and Carol L. Jusenius. 1976. "Economists' Approaches to Sex Segregation in the Labor Market: An Appraisal." Pp. 181–199 in Martha Blaxall and Barbara Reagan (eds.), *Women and the Workplace*. Chicago: University of Chicago Press.

Blau, Peter M. and Otis Dudley Duncan. 1967. *The American Occupational Structure*. New York: The Free Press.

Booth, Alan and John N. Edwards. 1985. "Age at Marriage and Marital Instability." *Journal of Marriage and the Family* 47:67–75.

Booth, Alan, David R. Johnson, Lynn White, and John N. Edwards. 1984. "Women, Outside Employment, and Marital Instability." *American Journal of Sociology* 90:567–583.

Bose, Christine. 1973. *Jobs and Gender: Sex and Occupational Prestige.* Baltimore: Johns Hopkins University Press.

_____ and Peter Rossi. 1983. "Gender and Jobs: Prestige Standings of Occupations as Affected by Gender." *American Sociological Review* 48:316–330.

Bridges, William P. and Richard A. Berk. 1974. "Determinants of White-Collar Income: An Evaluation of Equal Pay for Equal Work." *Social Science Research* 3:211–233.

Brown, Carol A., Roslyn Feldberg, Elizabeth M. Fox, and Janet Kohen. 1976. "Divorce: Chance of a New Lifetime." *Journal of Social Issues* 32:119–133.

Carmines, Edward G. and Richard A. Zeller. 1979. *Reliability and Validity Assessment*. Sage University Papers on Quantitative Applications in the Social Sciences, series no. 07–017. Beverly Hills, CA: Sage Publications.

Center for Human Resource Research. 1981. *The National Longitudinal Surveys Handbook, 1981*. Columbus, OH: The Ohio State University.

Cherlin, Andrew. 1980. "Postponing Marriage: The Influence of Young Women's Work Expectations." *Journal of Marriage and the Family* 42:355–365.

_____. 1981. *Marriage, Divorce, Remarriage*. Cambridge, MA: Harvard University Press.

Cohen, Jacob and Patricia Cohen. 1975. *Applied Multiple Regression/Correlation Analysis for the Behavioral Sciences*. New York: John Wiley and Sons.

Corcoran, Mary. 1979a. "Women's Experience, Labor Force Withdrawals and Women's Wages: Empirical Results Using the Panel Study on Income Dynamics." Pp. 216–245 in Cynthia Lloyd, Emily Andrews, and Curtis Gilroy (eds.), *Women in the Labor Market*. New York: Columbia University Press.

————. 1979b. "The Economic Consequences of Marital Dissolution for Women in the Middle Years." *Sex Roles* 5:343–353.

———— and Greg J. Duncan. 1979. "Work History, Labor Force Attachment, and Earnings Differences between the Races and Sexes." *The Journal of Human Resources* 14:3–20.

Coser, Rose and Gerald Rokoff. 1974. "Women in the Occupational World: Social Disruption and Conflict." Pp. 490–511 in Rose Coser (ed.), *The Family*. New York: St. Martin's Press.

Coverman, Shelley. 1983. "Gender, Domestic Labor Time, and Wage Inequality." *American Sociological Review* 43:623–637.

————. 1986. "Occupational Segmentation and Sex Differences in Earnings." *Research in Social Stratification and Mobility* 5:139–172.

———— and Alice Kemp. 1987. "The Labor Supply of Female Heads of Household: Comparison with Male Heads and Wives." *Sociological Inquiry* 57:32–53.

Cramer, James C. 1980. "Fertility and Female Employment: Problems of Causal Direction." *American Sociological Review* 45:167–190.

Dannefer, Dale. 1987. "Aging as Intracohort Differentiation: Accentuation, the Matthew Effect, and the Life Course." *Sociological Forum* 2:211–236.

Darian, Jean C. 1975. "Convenience of Work and the Job Constraint of Children." *Demography* 12:245–258.

DeJong, Peter Y., Milton J. Brawer, and Stanley S. Robin. 1971. "Patterns of Female Intergenerational Occupational Mobility: A Comparison with Male Patterns of Intergenerational Occupational Mobility." *American Sociological Review* 36:1033–1042.

Doeringer, Peter and Michael J. Piore. 1971. *Internal Labor Markets and Manpower Analysis*. Lexington, MA: D.C. Heath.

Dowd, Maureen. 1983. "Many Women in Poll Value Jobs as Much as Family Life." *New York Times* December 4:1,66.

Elder, Glen H. 1978. "Approaches to Social Change and the Family." Pp. S1-S38 in John Demos and Sarane S. Boocock (eds.), *Turning Points: Historical and Sociological Essays on the Family*. Chicago: University of Chicago Press.

———— and Jeffrey K. Liker. 1982. "Hard Times in Women's Lives: Historical Influences across Forty Years." *American Journal of Sociology* 88:241–269.

Espenshade, Thomas J. 1979. "The Economic Consequences of Divorce." *Journal of Marriage and the Family* 41:615–625.

———. 1985. "Marriage Trends in America: Estimates, Implications, and Underlying Causes." *Population and Development Review* 11:193–245.

Farley, Reynolds. 1984. *Blacks and Whites: Narrowing the Gap?* Cambridge, MA: Harvard University Press.

Featherman, David L. and Robert M. Hauser. 1976. "Sexual Inequalities and Socioeconomic Achievement in the U.S., 1962–1973." *American Sociological Review* 41:462–483.

Felmlee, Diane. 1984. "The Dynamics of Women's Job Mobility." *Work and Occupations* 11:259–281.

Fligstein, Neil, Alexander Hicks, and S. Philip Morgan. 1983. "Toward a Theory of Income Determination." *Work and Occupations* 10:289–306.

Floge, Liliane. 1986. "The Search for Day Care in Dual-Earner Families." Paper presented at Annual Meeting of the Society for the Study of Social Problems, New York.

Freeman, Richard B. and James L. Medoff. 1984. *What Do Unions Do?* New York: Basic Books.

Gerson, Kathleen. 1985. *Hard Choices: How Women Decide about Work, Career and Motherhood.* Berkeley and Los Angeles: University of California Press.

Glass, Jennifer, Sara McLanahan, and Aage Sorenson. 1983. "The Consequences of Divorce: Effects of Sample Selection Bias." Madison, WI: Center for Demography and Ecology, University of Wisconsin.

Greene, William H. and Aline O. Quester. 1982. "Divorce Risk and Wives' Labor Supply Behavior." *Social Science Quarterly* 63:16–27.

Grossman, Allyson S. 1977. "The Labor Force Patterns of Divorced and Separated Women." *Monthly Labor Review* 100:48–53.

Haggstrom, Gus W., Linda J. Waite, David Kanouse, and Thomas Blaschke. 1984. *Changes in the Lifestyles of New Parents.* Santa Monica, CA: Rand.

Halaby, Charles N. 1979. "Sexual Inequality in the Workplace: An Employer-specific Analysis of Pay Differentials." *Social Science Research* 8:79–104.

Hampton, Robert. 1975. "Marital Disruption: Some Social and Economic Consequences." Pp. 163–186 in Greg Duncan and James Morgan (eds.), *Five Thousand American Families—Patterns of Economic Progress*, Vol. 3. Ann Arbor: Institute for Social Research, University of Michigan.

Hannan, Michael T., Nancy Brandon Tuma, and Lyle P. Groenveld. 1977. "Income

and Marital Events: Evidence from an Income-Maintenance Experiment."
American Journal of Sociology 82:1186–1211.

Hanson, Sandra L. 1983. "A Family Life-Cycle Approach to the Socioeconomic
Attainment of Working Women." *Journal of Marriage and the Family*
45:323–338.

Harrell, Frank E., Jr. 1985. "The LOGIST Procedure." Pp. 269–292 in SAS
Institute, Inc. (ed.), *SUGI Supplemental Library User's Guide*. Cary, NC:
SAS Institute, Inc.

Haurin, Donald R. 1986. "Women's Labor Market Reactions to Family Disruptions,
Husband's Unemployment, and Husband's Disability." Pp. 73–86 in Lois B.
Shaw (ed.), *Midlife Women at Work*. Lexington, MA: Lexington Books.

Hauser, Robert M. 1980. "On 'Stratification in a Dual Economy' " (Comment on
Beck et al., ASR, October 1978). *American Sociological Review* 45:702–712.

Hawley, Clifford and William T. Bielby. 1978. "Research Uses of the National
Longitudinal Survey Data on Mature Women." Pp. 63–108 in U.S.
Department of Labor, *Proceedings of a Conference on the National
Longitudinal Surveys of Mature Women, Women's Changing Roles at Home
and on the Job*. Washington, DC: U.S. Department of Labor.

Heckman, James. 1974. "Shadow Prices, Market Wages, and Labor Supply."
Econometrica 42:679–694.

———. 1979. "Sample Selection Bias as a Specification Error." *Econometrica*
47:153–161.

Hill, Martha S. 1979. "The Wage Effects of Marital Status and Children." *Journal of
Human Resources* 14:579–594.

Hill, C. Russell and Frank P. Stafford. 1985. "Lifetime Fertility, Childcare and
Labor Supply." Pp. 565–597 in F. Thomas Juster and Frank P. Stafford
(eds.), *Time, Goods and Well-Being*. Ann Arbor: University of Michigan
Press.

Hirsch, Eric. 1980. "Dual Labor Market Theory: A Sociological Critique."
Sociological Inquiry 50:133–145.

Hodson, Randy. 1984. "Companies, Industries and the Measurement of Economic
Segmentation." *American Sociological Review* 49:335–348.

———. 1985. "Some Considerations Concerning the Functional Form of Earnings."
Social Science Research 14:374–394.

Hoffman, Saul. 1977. "Marital Instability and the Economic Status of Women."
Demography 14:67–76.

——— and John Holmes. 1976. "Husbands, Wives and Divorce." Pp. 23–75 in
Greg J. Duncan and James N. Morgan (eds.), *Five Thousand American*

Families— Patterns of Economic Progress, vol. 4. Ann Arbor, MI: University of Michigan.

Huber, Joan and Glenna Spitze. 1981. "Considering Divorce: An Expansion of Becker's Theory of Marital Instability." *American Journal of Sociology* 87:75–89.

Hudis, Paula M. 1976. "Commitment to Work and to Family: Marital-Status Differences in Women's Earnings." *Journal of Marriage and the Family* 38:267–278.

Hyman, Herbert. 1983. *Of Time and Widowhood.* Durham, NC: Duke University Press.

Kalleberg, Arne L. 1986. *America at Work: National Surveys of Employees and Employers.* New York: Social Science Research Council.

Kanter, Rosabeth. 1977a. *Men and Women of the Corporation.* New York: Basic Books.

———. 1977b. *Work and Family in the United States: A Critical Review and Agenda for Research and Policy.* New York: Russell Sage.

Karasek, Robert A., Joseph E. Schwartz, and Carl F. Pieper. 1983a. "Validation of Survey Instrument for Job-Related Cardiovascular Illness (Part I)." New York: Columbia University Department of Industrial Engineering and Operations Research.

———. 1983b. "Validation of Survey Instrument for Job-Related Cardiovascular Illness for Men and Women (Part II)." New York: Columbia University Department of Industrial Engineering and Operations Research.

Killingsworth, Mark R. 1983. *Labor Supply.* New York: Cambridge University Press.

Knottnerus, J. David. 1987. "Status Attainment Research and Its Image of Society." *American Sociological Review* 52:113–121.

Lopata, Helena A. and Kathleen F. Norr. 1980. "Changing Commitments of American Women to Work and Family Roles." *Social Security Bulletin* 43:3–14.

Macke, Anne S., Paula M. Hudis, and Don Larrick. 1978. "Sex-Role Attitudes and Employment among Women: Dynamic Models of Continuity and Change." Pp. 129–154 in U.S. Department of Labor, *Proceedings of a Conference on the National Longitudinal Surveys of Mature Women, Women's Changing Roles at Home and on the Job.* Washington, DC: U.S. Department of Labor.

Malkiel, Burton G. and Judith A. Malkiel. 1973. "Male-Female Pay Differentials in Professional Employment." *American Economic Review* 63:693–705.

McClendon, McKee J. 1976. "The Occupational Status Attainment Processes of Males and Females." *American Sociological Review* 41:52–64.

Medoff, James L. and Katharine G. Abraham. 1980. "Experience, Performance and Earnings." *The Quarterly Journal of Economics* 95:703–736.

_____. 1981. "Are Those Paid More Really More Productive? The Case of Experience." *Journal of Human Resources* 16:186–216.

Mincer, Jacob and Solomon Polachek. 1974. "Family Investments in Human Capital: Earnings of Women." *Journal of Political Economy* 82:S76–S108.

Moen, Phyllis. 1986. "Women's Life Transitions in the Middle Years: A Longitudinal Analysis." Paper presented at Annual Meeting of the American Sociological Association, New York.

_____ and Ken R. Smith. 1986. "Women at Work: Commitment and Behavior over the Life Course." *Sociological Forum* 3:450–475.

Moore, Sylvia F. 1979. *The Short-Term Effects of Marital Disruption on the Labor Supply Behavior of Young Women*. Columbus, OH: The Ohio State University Press.

Mortimer, Jeylan T., Richard Hall, and Reuben Hill. 1978. "Husbands' Occupational Attributes as Constraints on Wives' Employment." *Sociology of Work and Occupations* 5:285–313.

Mosteller, Frederick and John W. Tukey. 1977. *Data Analysis and Regression*. Reading, MA: Addison-Wesley.

Mott, Frank L. 1978. "The NLS Mature Women's Cohort: A Socioeconomic Overview." Pp. 23–61 in U.S. Department of Labor, *Proceedings of a Conference on the National Longitudinal Surveys of Mature Women, Women's Changing Roles at Home and on the Job*. Washington, DC: U.S. Department of Labor.

_____ and Sylvia F. Moore. 1979. "The Causes of Marital Disruption among Young American Women: An Interdisciplinary Perspective." *Journal of Marriage and Family* 41:355–365.

Nestel, Gilbert, Jacqueline Mercier, and Lois B. Shaw. 1983. "Economic Consequences of Midlife Change in Marital Status." Pp. 109–125 in Lois B. Shaw (ed.), *Unplanned Careers: The Working Lives of Middle-aged Women*. Lexington, MA: Lexington Books.

Norton, Arthur J. and Jeanne E. Moorman. 1987. "Current Trends in Marriage and Divorce among American Women." *Journal of Marriage and the Family* 49:3–14.

O'Neill, June. 1985. "The Trend in the Male–Female Wage Gap in the United States." *Journal of Labor Economics* 3:S91–S116.

Oppenheimer, Valerie Kincade. 1970. *The Female Labor Force in the United States: Demographic Factors Governing Its Growth and Changing Composition.* Berkeley and Los Angeles: University of California Press.

————. 1982. *Work and the Family.* New York: Academic Press.

Parnes, Herbert S., Carol L. Jusenius, Francine Blau, Gilbert Nestel, Richard L. Shortlidge, Jr., and Steven Sandell. 1976. *Dual Careers: A Longitudinal Analysis of the Labor Market Experience of Women.* R & D Monograph 21, vol. 4. Washington, DC: U.S. Department of Labor.

Pear, Robert. 1983. "Earnings Gap Is Narrowing Slightly for Women." *New York Times* October 3:B15.

————. 1984. "Wage Lag Is Found for White Women." *New York Times* January 16:A1.

Perrucci, Carolyn C. 1978. "Income Attainment of College Graduates: A Comparison of Employed Women and Men." *Sociology and Social Research* 62:361–386.

Peters, Elizabeth. 1986. "Factors Affecting Remarriage." Pp. 99–114 in Lois B. Shaw (ed.), *Midlife Women at Work.* Lexington, MA: Lexington Books.

Peterson, Richard R. 1987. "The Effect of Divorce on Wages of Working Women." *Research in Social Stratification and Mobility* 6:61–74.

Pfeffer, Jeffrey and Jerry Ross. 1982. "The Effects of Marriage and a Working Wife on Occupational and Wage Attainment." *Administrative Science Quarterly* 27:66–80.

Plateris, Alexander. 1979. *Divorces by Marriage Cohort* (Vital and Health Statistics Series 21, no. 34). Hyattsville, MD: National Center for Health Statistics.

Polachek, Solomon W. 1975. "Discontinuous Labor Force Participation and Its Effect on Women's Market Earnings." Pp. 90–122 in Cynthia Lloyd (ed.), *Sex, Discrimination and the Division of Labor.* New York: Columbia University Press.

Priebe, John, Joan Heinkel, and Stanley Greene. 1972. *1970 Occupation and Industry Classification Systems in Terms of Their 1960 Occupation and Industry Elements* (Technical Paper no. 26). Washington, DC: U.S. Bureau of the Census.

Rhoton, Patricia. 1984. *Attrition and the National Longitudinal Surveys of Labor Market Experience: Avoidance, Control and Correction.* Columbus, OH: Center for Human Resource Research, The Ohio State University.

Robinson, Robert V. and Jonathan Kelley. 1979. "Class as Conceived by Marx and Dahrendorf: Effects on Income Inequality, Class Consciousness, and Class Conflict in the United States and Great Britain." *American Sociological Review* 44:38–58.

Roos, Patricia. 1981. "Sex Stratification in the Workplace: Male-Female Differences in Economic Returns to Occupation." *Social Science Research* 10:195–224.

———. 1983. "Marriage and Women's Occupational Attainment in Cross-cultural Perspective." *American Sociological Review* 48:852–864.

———. 1985. *Gender and Work: A Comparative Analysis of Industrial Societies.* Albany: State University of New York Press.

Rosenbaum, James. 1984. *Career Mobility in a Corporate Hierarchy.* New York: Academic Press.

Salvo, Joseph J. and John M. McNeil. 1984. "Lifetime Work Experience and Its Effect on Earnings: Retrospective Data from the 1979 Income Survey Development Program." U.S. Bureau of the Census, *Current Population Reports* Series P-23, number 136. Washington, DC: USGPO.

Sandell, Steven H. and David Shapiro. 1978. "An Exchange: The Theory of Human Capital and the Earnings of Women—A Re-examination of the Evidence." *Journal of Human Resources* 13:103–117.

Scharf, Lois. 1980. *To Work and to Wed: Female Employment, Feminism, and the Great Depression.* Westport, CT: Greenwood Press.

Schwartz, Joseph E. 1979. "Individual Earnings and Family Income." Pp. 231–250 in Christopher Jencks (ed.), *Who Gets Ahead?* New York: Basic Books.

——— and Carl F. Pieper. 1982. "A Method for Analyzing the Effects of Working Conditions on Health." Paper presented at Center for the Social Sciences, Columbia University, New York (February 15).

Shaw, Lois. 1978. "Economic Consequences of Marital Disruption." Pp. 181–203 in U.S. Department of Labor, *Proceedings of a Conference on the National Longitudinal Surveys of Mature Women, Women's Changing Roles at Home and on the Job.* Washington, DC: U.S. Department of Labor.

Siebert, W.S. and P.J. Sloane. 1981. "The Measurement of Sex and Marital Status Discrimination at the Workplace." *Economica* 48:125–141.

Smith Ralph E. 1979. "The Movement of Women into the Labor Force." Pp. 1–29 in Ralph E. Smith (ed.), *The Subtle Revolution: Women at Work.* Washington: Urban Institute.

Sokoloff, Natalie J. 1980. *Between Money and Love.* New York: Praeger.

Sorensen, Aage. 1983. "Sociological Research on the Labor Market." *Work and Occupations* 10:261–287.

South, Scott J. and Glenna Spitze. 1986. "Determinants of Divorce over the Marital Life Course." *American Sociological Review* 51:583–590.

Spilerman, Seymour. 1977. "Careers, Labor Market Structures, and Socioeconomic Achievement." *American Journal of Sociology* 83:551–593.

Stolzenberg, Ross M. 1978. "Bringing the Boss Back in: Employer Size, Employee Schooling, and Socioeconomic Achievement." *American Sociological Review* 43:813–828.

Suter, Larry E. and Herman P. Miller. 1973. "Income Differences between Men and Career Women." *American Journal of Sociology* 78:962–974.

Sweet, James A. 1973. *Women in the Labor Force*. New York: Seminar Press.

Talbert, Joan and Christine E. Bose. 1977. "Wage-Attainment Processes: The Retail Clerk Case." *American Journal of Sociology* 83:403–424.

Thornton, Arland, Duane Alwin, and Donald Camburn. 1983. "Causes and Consequences of Sex-Role Attitudes and Attitude Change." *American Sociological Review* 48:211–227.

Tienda, Marta, Shelley Smith, and Vilma Ortiz. 1987. "Industrial Restructuring, Gender Segregation, and Sex Differences in Earnings." *American Sociological Review* 52:195–210.

Tolbert, Charles, Patrick M. Horan, and E.M. Beck. 1980. "The Structure of Economic Segmentation: A Dual Economy Approach." *American Journal of Sociology* 85:1095–1116.

Treiman, Donald J. and Heidi I. Hartmann. 1981. *Women, Work, and Wages: Equal Pay for Jobs of Equal Value*. Washington, DC: National Academy Press.

Treiman, Donald J. and Kermit Terrell. 1975. "Sex and the Process of Status Attainment: A Comparison of Working Women and Men." *American Sociological Review* 40:174–200.

Tukey, John W. 1977. *Exploratory Data Analysis*. Reading, MA: Addison-Wesley.

U.S. Bureau of the Census. 1967. *Marital and Family Status, March 1966* (Current Population Reports, Series P-20, no. 159). Washington, DC: USGPO.

————. 1970. *Census of Population: 1970, Detailed Characteristics*. United States Summary. Washington, DC: USGPO.

————. 1976. *Number, Timing and Duration of Marriages and Divorces in the United States: June 1975* (Current Population Reports Series P-20, no. 297). Washington, DC: USGPO.

————. 1980. *Population Profile of the United States* (Current Population Reports, Series P-20, no. 350). Washington, DC: USGPO.

————. 1985a. *Statistical Abstract of the United States: 1986*. Washington, DC: USGPO.

_____. 1985b. *Marital Status and Living Arrangements: March 1985* (Current Population Reports, Series P-20, no. 410). Washington, DC: USGPO.

U.S. Bureau of Labor Statistics. 1980. *Employment and Earnings*, January.

_____. 1981. *Half of Nation's Children Have Working Mothers*. Washington, DC: U.S. Department of Labor.

_____. 1983. *Handbook of Labor Statistics*. Bulletin No. 2175. Washington, DC: U.S. Department of Labor.

_____. 1984. *Families at Work: The Jobs and the Pay*. Bulletin No. 2209. Washington, DC: U.S. Department of Labor.

U.S. Department of Labor. 1980. *Perspectives on Working Women: A Databook* (Bulletin 2080). Washington, DC: USGPO.

Waite, Linda J. 1978. "Projecting Female Labor Force Participation from Sex-Role Attitudes." *Social Science Research* 7:299–318.

_____, Gus W. Haggstrom, and David E. Kanouse. 1985. "Changes in the Employment Activities of New Parents." *American Sociological Review* 50:263–272.

_____ and Paula M. Hudis. 1980. *The Development and Maintenance of a Segregated Labor Force*. Santa Monica, CA: The Rand Corporation.

Wallace, Michael and Arne Kalleberg. 1981. "Economic Organization of Firms and Labor Market Consequences: Toward a Specification of Dual Economy Theory." Pp. 77–117 in Ivar Berg (ed.), *Sociological Perspectives on Labor Markets*. New York: Academic Press.

Wanner, Richard and Lionel Lewis. 1983. "Economic Segmentation and the Course of the Occupational Career." *Work and Occupations* 10:307–324.

Weiss, Robert S. 1975. *Marital Separation*. New York: Basic Books.

_____. 1984. "The Impact of Marital Dissolution on Income and Consumption in Single-Parent Households." *Journal of Marriage and the Family* 46:115–127.

Weitzman, Lenore. 1985. *The Divorce Revolution*. New York: The Free Press.

Index